50 Law of Attraction Exercises, Tips & Tricks To Hack Your Mind & Increase Your Manifestation Power

Jessica Connor, Ph.D.

i

Printed in the United States of America

ISBN-13: 978-1541152281

Contents

Foreword

Within each of our minds is a skillful storyteller. This storyteller can either be an immense asset to helping our dreams manifest into reality, or it can be a huge demotivating force that keeps us stuck in unwanted circumstances. It tells us stories on a consistent basis about everything, and can be programmed to influence and encourage us towards our dreams. We have full control over this storyteller once we become aware of it and begin to make choices to arrange only positive accounts and reinforce them on a regular basis. Those who are successful at making their dreams a reality are masters at monitoring the storyteller within them. They use it to their advantage to engage with the types of outer conditions they deliberately choose for themselves.

Life itself is also very interesting. It is a swirling, vibrating mass of energy in various configurations that is always changing. This energy, perceived via your senses, is edited within your brain using the programming of your subconscious mind. What you perceive is merely a representation of reality, as viewed by you. Your experiences are the brain's depiction of reality as dictated by your subconscious mind. The subconscious mind is not much different than a machine. And this machine, generally speaking, is resistant to change; otherwise, your reality would alter as frequently as you encounter a different thought.

Possibly due to some of the current ambiguous law of attraction material available, many people experience difficulty when trying to implement correct techniques to manifest their desires. This can create frustrated attempts for those aiming to attract their life intentionally; and failed efforts lead to a belief that the law of attraction doesn't work. It can be tricky to understand how to govern the power you hold, so you will need to learn to master your mind and the current habits it possesses for optimal results.

This book is written with the purpose of increasing the manifestation potential within those that choose to deliberately create an existence of detailed selection. This is not only possible to accomplish, but probable with the proper tools and precise dedication. There is a great deal of information on how and why the law of attraction works, but not a lot of instruction on the ways in which to truly employ practices that create results. With these exercises, transcending limitations can be easier than you may currently believe to be true.

The first portion of the book provides a simple introduction to subconscious reasoning for a better understanding of your current conditions and circumstances. This is followed by 10 simple tips to begin changing any undesired results; these are what I refer to as the basics. You may already be acquainted with some of these basic processes; however, they are worth repeating as foundational information and to stress their importance.

Following the basic information are an additional 40 (not-so-common) exercises, tips and tricks that are very practical and easy to implement in everyday life. If you are well-versed in basic law of attraction principles, you may want to begin with this section on page 37. Each process is designed to shift your mindset from focusing on daily routine, and to unlock the subconscious powerhouse that carries a whole new world of possibilities for you. Unless you open the gift box you've been provided with, you can never receive the present inside. The intention of these writings is to show you how to do that. This book was created to assist you in the creation of new beliefs of your choosing and faith in your ability to manifest what you desire.

If some of these exercises seem unusual to you, realize that your mind has a very rigid set of rules and guidelines that it follows each day in order to keep its routine as normal as possible. To create new results in your life, a new set of boundaries must be established. Stepping out of the comfort zone is often required to accomplish new outcomes. Individual results will be dependent upon the ability to be consistent enough to create new habits. Happy Manifesting!

1

Understanding Your Subconscious Mind

The most prominent reason people fail to become masters of the power of their mind, and therefore their outer conditions, is because they don't understand how the subconscious thinks. Since our true power comes from our subconscious mind, it's essential to comprehend the differences between its role and the conscious mind's role. If your intention is to use your mind to attract something, or change something about yourself, it's imperative to utilize the proper methods of delicately aligning with the subconscious mind's massive potential regarding life in general. To alter results, we must access the subconscious being itself in such a way that allows it to cooperate and change any underlying directives or hidden decisions.

Far more capable than any macro computer, the subconscious stores every event, occurrence, emotion and circumstance. Subconscious programming happens very early. Most of this programming occurs between birth and 7 years old, but we are still programming our subconscious mind well until the age of 16. Children between 0 and 7 years old are learning more on a subconscious level than they do on a conscious level. All of that data is stored and is available for recall as we navigate our life's circumstances. This portion of the mind contains all of the reasons you do what you do, and believe what you believe. If you can't seem to change your mindset, or make a desired change in life, the key will be held your subconscious mind.

This subconscious does not work on logic. Likened to a video recorder, it doesn't judge or analyze; it simply tapes as it sees and hears. It also doesn't make any distinctions between right and wrong, or good and bad, when storing beliefs. What many people fail to realize about the subconscious mind is its vast complexity and potential. It's open for business and constantly working, absorbing information in the background even we're not paying attention. It is a guardian and a gate keeper, using the data stored from events to deduct likely probabilities, and prompt us accordingly. It rules the five senses, involuntary muscles, emotions and intuition, and is also responsible for communicating with the Higher Self to manifest everyday reality. Its capacity is virtually unlimited.

Often, we will drift into an "automatic" mode of reaction, based purely on subconscious instincts. The subconscious has no choice but to run as a default program unless told otherwise. The hindrance for most people that make the decision to consciously create their life in a deliberate manner is that they fail to make a full impression on the subconscious mind regarding their wish. They must untwist engrained facts that don't serve them, and replace them with ones that do to achieve desired results. As a person becomes more aware of the role of the subconscious, and they are able to get in tune with its programming, they can re-program it in a new direction guided by conscious awareness instead of social, parental, or any other type of past programming.

Have you ever wondered why it's difficult for people to change beliefs? It's because the subconscious mind can distort facts, alter perception or even let you see things that don't exist just to support what it has already established as fact. As an example, people who think that others don't like them can actually perceive other people's facial expressions in a way that confirms their beliefs. It's very normal for a person who doesn't think that people like him to mistakenly interpret a look or a gesture in such a way that further constructs his negative beliefs about himself. The subconscious mind carries the role of seeking out ways to establish truth and correctness, and does so in an uninterrupted and automatic fashion.

In addition, objects we observe are first rendered in our brains before we fully see them. During that process, the subconscious mind can interfere to let us see things differently. For example, a person who fears snakes can think that a wooden stick is a snake even for few seconds before he realizes it's just a wooden stick. In instances where checking whether the object really exists or not isn't possible, the person might live with an incorrect perception of reality throughout life.

Most importantly, the subconscious mind is constantly communicating with the Universe based on our programmed inner emotions. It is in an "always on" mode with this formless substance; this divinity. It works day and night to make your behavior fit a pattern consistent with your emotionalized thoughts. Based on programming, combined with the Universal law of vibration that states we are like a tuning fork consistently sending signals out, people, events and circumstances are attracted to our lives without our conscious awareness. This is why tragedy often comes from nowhere for some, and conversely others seem to have a perpetual rabbit's foot in their pocket.

This connection between the subconscious and the Universe rewards us continuously with the very things we transmit out. You attract what you are, not what you want. For this reason, those who have had difficult upbringings, or early childhood and pre-teen trauma, should be especially aware of the following processes and work diligently to reprogram their subconscious mind so they can attract those things they now choose to have in their lives.

Although these facts may make it seem as though the subconscious mind is working against us, its most basic function is rooted in survival. It will do whatever it takes to ensure our safety, even to the unintentional detriment of creating, and re-creating, negative life circumstances. It will always gravitate to what it knows, not what is best for you, because it likes known quantities. Unknowns are seen as scary to the subconscious mind, because it cannot calculate a known outcome with an unknown variable.

Because of this, many people tend to repeat thoughts and behaviors. They will stay in the same undesirable relationship, unwanted job or always go down any familiar path because it is what they know and their mind understands the end result. Directives based on early survival decisions or genetic influences take utmost priority. When someone makes a new decision while trying to overcome or replace a subconscious survival directive, the result can be self-sabotage and failure based on this.

Fortunately, we have the conscious gift of free-will and choice. However, consciously controlling the subconscious mind is not something that can be done with force or coercion. The act of consciously applying willpower sends signals of struggle to the subconscious mind, therefore creating resistance. In addition, the subconscious mind reads our emotions just as intricately as our thoughts. If these two are congruent, then the subconscious mind accepts the idea or thought as fact. This is true whether regarding something that is positive, or negative; the subconscious mind doesn't know the difference. What matters most is that thoughts, mental images and emotions are all in alignment. This sets the subconscious mind into action to make our ideas happen.

The human mind is undoubtedly an underutilized powerhouse, and is vastly untapped. An average individual uses less than 10% of his or her mind's ability. Accordingly, you should clearly understand that you can tap the power of your mind for your personal development. Whatever we desire to attract and create must be impressed upon the subjective or subconscious mind with proper methods and consistency.

You are designed to do more than just survive. With conscious action and alignment, this mechanism also has the ability to ensure that you thrive. This portion of the mind was originated to be open to your direct influence, and ideally the two minds, conscious and subconscious, are created to work together for your benefit. Your subconscious mind has been waiting for you to take conscious charge of your life, on a consistent basis, ever since you've had the cognitive abilities to do so, which for most is between 20 and 25 years of age.

Any emotional suffering you may experience in life is generated to prompt pause and reflection, and to suggest making inner changes. It is a byproduct of not accepting that you are wired to face that pain which has the capacity to stretch you out of comfortable places that obstruct evolving. In other words, you are wired with a tendency to resist change until the pain of not changing becomes greater than changing. Your mind seeks to impart its wisdom to you, and pain is one of its messengers.

As in any healthy relationship, we each need to learn how to communicate effectively with our inner self in ways that build rapport, foster compassion, understanding, acceptance and honor, and create the sense of safety required to remain empathically connected to ourselves and life around us.

2

10 Tips to Become a Master of Your Subconscious Mind

In this chapter you'll find 10 tips to begin consciously mastering your mind power. It may be that you aware of, or even practice, many of the points noted here. Most individuals that are well-informed in law of attraction principles undoubtedly will have some understanding of the basics such as visualization, affirmations and meditation. However, it may be worth your while to study these tips and the information given to solidify your knowledge, as well as to get a grasp on the reasoning and importance of executing these actions in a precise manner. If you feel that you are sufficiently skilled in these concepts, move ahead to chapter 3 to begin implementing the exercises offered.

1: Tip - _Risk Taking_

Superior men and women are always stretching themselves and reaching outside of their comfort zones. They are very aware how quickly the comfort zone, in any area, can become a rut. They know that complacency is the great enemy of creativity and future possibilities. As it was previously mentioned that unknowns are seen as scary to the subconscious mind, risk becomes an important factor to success. This facilitates change by overriding existing standards.

To create change in your subconscious patterning, you must allow for an unknown variable -- something different than what the mind is already aware of. The mind thinks it knows everything. And, in a way it does. It knows everything it knows. It may even know everything that is possible; but, it must believe in those possibilities on an individual basis.

If you want a new life, you must challenge your subconscious mind by making it seek out new variables. Be willing to feel awkward and uncomfortable doing new things the first few times. Your subconscious mind causes you to feel emotionally and physically uncomfortable whenever you attempt to do anything new or different, or to change any of your established patterns of behavior. However, risk-taking pushes the boundaries and creates advanced, expanded comfort zones in the subconscious mind.

There is a common misconception that taking risks can be detrimental. The truth of the matter is, taking risks is no more risky than playing it safe or maintaining the status quo. In fact, often by failing to innovate, make changes and move forward in different areas of our lives, we open ourselves up to the possibility of stagnation and falling behind. Without risk-taking, the opportunity for growth beyond what is already being experienced is dramatically diminished. Risk offers new causes that set into motion new effects.

With risk-taking, there is always the possibility of making mistakes or even failing to get desired results with the attempt. However, the most successful people in the world understand that failing is what ultimately propels them to achieve their goals. It's their perception of so-called failure that differs from most. Failure is ok with them because they understand the rewards in their effort. If one risk doesn't work out for them, they consider a new risk rather than taking permanent defeat; consequently, this alters the boundaries of their subconscious patterning.

With this type of action and attitude, the subconscious mind has no choice but to concede to the fact that the conscious mind has rigidly decided that it will continue repeating attempts until it is successful. Once this type of surrender occurs within the subconscious, existing limits are replaced with larger and grander standards that attract new outcomes in alignment with the conscious request.

#2: Tip - _Auto-Inquisition_

One powerful way to change the subconscious mind is by asking it questions. Questions allow for those unknown variables already mentioned, and open the mind to seek new answers. The subconscious is designed to help you get an answer or solve a problem you are having difficulty with using the quickest, fastest way to the solution. It works on the principle of least effort and follows the path of least resistance. This is, once again, to ensure your survival.

Can you ignore a question? Can you ignore this one? It should be noted that your subconscious mind answered each of those questions before you ever consciously created a response. The brain cannot ignore a question; it must process the question into an answer before it even considers that the question is a question. This is something we can use to our advantage.

The trick is to format the questions in a precise way in order to get by the subconscious mind's walls. A style of question that allows for this is: "What else is possible that I have not yet considered?" With a question like this, the subconscious mind must automatically go in search of something unknown because it has already considered every possibility it is aware of. And, it will continue to search until it finds the answer.

Phrasing questions regarding your desires triggers the subconscious to seek the answers immediately. Examples might be: "How cool is it that I have so much money?" "What am I going to do with all of this extra cash?" "What do I need to get ahead in life?" "How can I make this a reality?" Your subconscious mind cannot disregard these questions. It immediately processes and attempts to answer any queries. While you may not consciously come up with the answer, your brain has already answered the question, and your subconscious is holding the response for you.

The subconscious mind also relates to "what if" style questions. For example, "What if I were successful at my goals? What would that look like?" When we keep asking questions, and stay in search of more questions, we are able to create more change in our lives. Through subconscious answer seeking, the mind comes to conclusions that open the possibility of further growth. Constantly challenging your subconscious mind with the "What else is possible" and "What if" style of inquiries will keep it on its metaphoric toes in order to create desired results.

This technique, which can be formatted in whatever way works best for you, is known as auto-inquisition. It was used by musicians such as Ludwig Beethoven, J.S. Bach and also by Thomas Edison and many other inventors. Thomas Edison practiced auto-inquisition by sitting in his favorite chair and lightly resting while holding metal balls in his hand suspended over a metal bowl. During this rest, he would focus on a question about a problem he was trying to solve.

The moment he started to doze off, his hand would relax and the balls would clang into the metal bowl, waking him up. This allowed Edison to remain suspended between the sleeping and dreaming states where he would have access to information in his subconscious mind. This particular drowsy state, combined with auto-inquisition, is an ideal creative playground that has the power to manifest solutions with phenomenal accuracy.

To increase your success rate with auto-inquisition, asking questions just prior to sleep, as you're in a relaxed state and just about to drift off, will amplify the outcome. The function of your subconscious mind is to store and retrieve data and many people awake after falling asleep with a question in mind to find that the answer to the next step towards their goal has miraculously been delivered.

#3: Tip - *Empowering Thoughts and Precision Affirmations*

Remember that your subconscious mind is constantly eavesdropping on every conscious thought and conversation you have with yourself or others. Therefore, choose empowering thoughts and precise affirmations. When you wholeheartedly believe positive, precise affirmations about your personal acumen and abilities, your brain will imprint these beliefs into new neural pathways and create the desired outcomes.

The finest method of tapping into the unlimited power of your subconscious mind is to become knowledgeable of what's genuinely going on inside your conscious mind. Very few people bother about what they're thinking of during the course of a day, permitting random thoughts to pass through their minds. On the contrary, successful people exercise tremendous control over their thoughts. You have the ability to favorably utilize the law of attraction within your subconscious mind when you choose and control your thoughts intentionally.

Thinking is usually a mixture of words, sentences, mental images and sensations. Thoughts are visitors that call on the central station of the mind. They come, stay a while, and then disappear, making space for other thoughts. Some of these thoughts stay longer, gain power, and affect the life of the person thinking them. It is of vital importance to be careful of what goes into the subconscious mind. Words and thoughts that are repeated will get stronger through repetition, sink into the subconscious mind and affect the behavior, actions and reactions of the person involved, as well as outer conditions and circumstances.

The subconscious mind regards the words and thoughts that get lodged inside it as expressing and describing a real situation, and therefore endeavors to align the words and thoughts with reality. It works diligently to make these words and thoughts actual existence in the life of the person saying or thinking them. If you consciously choose the thoughts, phrases and words that you repeat in your mind, your life will start to change. You will begin creating new situations and circumstances through the power of affirmations.

Affirmations are sentences that are repeated often during the day, and which sink into the subconscious mind, thereby releasing its enormous power to materialize the intention of the words and phrases in the outside world. This does not mean that every word you utter will bring results. In order to trigger the subconscious mind into action, the words have to be said with attention, intention and with feeling.

To obtain positive results with this method, affirmations must be phrased in positive wording. The subconscious mind has a difficult time processing negatives, like the words don't and not. If I tell you don't think of a pink elephant, what are you thinking about? Most likely, it's a pink elephant. In everyday life, many say things such as, "I don't like my financial situation," and the subconscious can only see and hear, "I like my financial situation." This is the reason to make sure affirmations and daily thoughts are structured in a positive way. It's also the exact reason why talking about what we "don't" want will often manifest. The negative word "don't" is cancelled out by the subconscious mind, leaving only the unwanted thing to be created.

When your goals are embedded properly, they activate the law of expectation within your subconscious mind. These are fresh beliefs about what is truly possible for you to accomplish. Accordingly, this initiates the law of emotion and the law of correspondence inside your subconscious mind. Consequently, your energy level is increased dramatically, and your creativity is stimulated in a significant manner.

#4: Tip – <u>Repetition</u>

One of the great rules the subconscious mind follows is that the beliefs it holds are created and grow stronger through repetition. Repetition can take various forms such as reading the belief, listening to it, visualizing it or mentally affirming it. Combined with emotion and sensation, repetition is the catalyst of all subconscious change. In order to create new beliefs, thoughts and affirmations must be consistently repeated as a means of developing new auto-pilot behaviors.

Do you remember when you first learned to drive a car? It took the utmost concentration and conscious action to operate the vehicle in a way that ensured your safety and accuracy. Every second was spent focusing on how to drive effectively. Eventually, with repetition and conscious direction, driving a vehicle becomes automatic. The subconscious brain takes over in a, "Now I know what to do, you can relax" kind of way. Eventually, it becomes a subconscious action whereby your mind drifts into a dream state while your body takes you to your destination without even a second thought.

This is exactly how the subconscious mind works with all established behavior. If your behavior and beliefs are not conducive of the results you seek, you have the option to consciously change them. However, the subconscious mind must take this directive with consistent, practiced repetition until it becomes automatic. In addition, the cells in your body have the ability to learn many daily actions, thus taking over many functions from the mind. They take direction from your subconscious mind to ensure they are in alignment with requests that relate to beliefs. This part of the mind makes certain that your behavior and physical body respond exactly the way you are programmed. Through repetition, new programming can replace outdated modes of conducting oneself.

Similar to building the body's muscles through regular visits to the gym, your mental muscles require the same repetitive, consistent dedication for long-lasting shifts in the mind. The results must go from conscious thinking, to habitual thinking, to automatic subconscious understanding. Every person is different; however, repetition generally becomes automatic between the 60 and 90 day mark. Some people are able to change their automatic behavior in 30 days, while others may need up to 6 months or longer. The key is to remain consistent until you realize your new behavior is automatic.

#5: Tip - <u>Autosuggestion</u>

Autosuggestion is a form of self-induced suggestion wherein the thoughts, feelings, or behavior of an individual are guided by oneself. It goes one step beyond positive affirmations. Affirmations are broad in structure, while autosuggestion techniques bypass your thinking mind and awareness of your material body and are used to affirm your unique human spirit. It is in essence the quiet chatter we say to ourselves, about ourselves. And when we are talking to ourselves, we are talking to our subconscious mind.

While your conscious mind is your logical, rational and analytical mind, your subconscious is your illogical, irrational, non-analytical mind. It will believe something whether it makes logical sense or not. It never questions what you tell it with accuracy. Autosuggestion is a great tool for effectively molding the subconscious mind to attract desires by stating what you choose to be. Once again, this requires consistent repetition.

Whether you realize it or not, you have probably been using autosuggestion techniques your whole life. If you have ever suggested to yourself that you are rich, poor, fat, skinny, lucky, unlucky, or so on, you have used autosuggestion. To use this most effectively for the things you desire, put yourself into a deeply relaxed state. If you know self-hypnosis or meditation techniques that do this for you, use those. If not, simply close your eyes and follow your breath going in and out for a few minutes while counting backwards from twenty to one.

Practice using "I AM" statements that positively reflect the new you. This states your suggestion in the present moment and in the first person, and centers you at the precise moment of the suggestion. Give your entire attention to the autosuggestions, repeating them over and over again. Examples might be: "I am abundant in all areas of life," "I am a magnet for positive experiences" or "I am the luckiest person I know."

When these self affirmations are stated on a regular basis, they eventually sink into the subconscious mind and are taken at face value. Positive words and sentences regarding the nature of the self have the ability to change your inner world, create new beliefs, alter vibrations and in due time change your reality. New brain waves begin to be created and the working structure of your brain starts a process of permanent change. After years of research, neuroscientists have found that when we send new information to the brain, new communication paths between the neurons are created. The brain can then shape and manifest a new existence.

#6: *Tip - Visualization and Imagination*

Fortunately, the subconscious does not know the difference between what is real and what is imagined. You have the choice to consciously control your subjective mind because of this. If your intention is to use any of the methods mentioned, always imagine you are doing so in the NOW. The subconscious mind will never disagree with you, believe you don't have it, or believe you haven't made the change when visualization is implemented correctly.

The subconscious mind does not work with language, but with imagery, sound, taste, smell, touch, sight and emotions. Thought,

24

sensation and emotion are the sum of all our experience. This is how the mind records and relates to any event. Imagine touching a hot stove, and how that would feel on your hand. Or, when you think of the word lemon you may see a lemon, or perhaps can even feel, smell or taste it. This is your subconscious working for you. Notice how effortless this is.

To reiterate the point, your subconscious mind cannot tell the difference between imagination and reality. Consequently, the more specific you are able to make your visualizations, the more information you feed to your subconscious mind. This causes positive behavioral change. Our conscious mind has a tendency to focus on and visualize past events, and these can often be negative. Visualizing your end result in the present time, with all of the sensation and feeling you are able to create, subtly tricks your subconscious mind into believing it is actually happening.

The subconscious is able to focus on the bigger picture and isn't limited to only what has happened before. What this means is, if you are able to genuinely "see" yourself as successful in your mind, your subconscious will process that as reality. Athletes are the most notable group to use visualization as a tool to perform better, but any one of us can do the same. Visualization is so powerful, in fact, that according to psycho-neuromuscular theory your muscles can actually get stronger just by visualizing using them as so.

During visualization, get into a relaxed and comfortable state. Imagine what your life looks like with all of your wishes and wants in place for you. It's important to focus only on the end result that you desire, without any thought as to how it happened. Put yourself in the visualization, seeing it from a first person point of view, rather than watching yourself. Most importantly, train your mind to incorporate all of the feeling states that you can during your visualization process. Smell the air, see the environment and the people you are with, touch objects, feel your gait as you walk, taste your favorite food, hear the sounds around you. As mentioned, your subconscious mind speaks the language of feeling fluently. The more you are able to integrate these sensations during this process, the more your subconscious mind will begin to seek out its actualization and manifestation.

#7: Tip - *Expectation*

The power of expectation subconsciously controls your life to create self-fulfilling prophesies. Expectation serves as the master plan for your subconscious mind. Your belief that you are a particular kind of person, with a particular role, generates the expectations which can make you successful, or unsuccessful. Expectations can fill you with the energy to achieve more, or make you unhappy and dissatisfied. Unfortunately, the expectations of many people are narrowed by their early experiences in life. However, if you want to

26

make positive changes regarding your reality, discovering ways to change your expectations is a powerful component.

Your subconscious mind remembers thousands of your habitual activities suggested to be stored by the brain as instantly retrievable. All nerve cells recognize combinational patterns. Any cells that are unrelated to your current concern become inhibited, since they fail to recognize a linking pattern. Throughout the nervous system there are neural circuits which switch off other circuits when their own areas are energized. As a result, context is identified through elimination. Everything you do works this way. For each word in your speech, this system eliminates all the words in your vocabulary which do not suit the expression of your idea. Accordingly, this same mechanism can narrow your range of expectations unless challenged with repetition to create new ones.

It may become taxing for the mind to stay in a place of positive expectation when it finds itself in a "perceived" negative life situation. Being the survival machine it is, it often will come to some negative projection or assumption about the situation. This is where it's important to have a depth in your being that allows you to stay open to the mind's movements without being totally identified with it. This space keeps your vibration from being totally influenced by the negativity of the mind and thus ensures room to allow new expectations and solutions to develop without coercion.

Begin to change your expectations into more desirable anticipations through eliminating any reinforcement of negative assumptions that your mind delivers to you. Simply allow these assumptions to be as they are, and then allow them to leave the same way -- without any attachment to them, negative or positive. The best attitude to have is to never come to a negative conclusion about anything happening, rather just see everything as a step towards a more positive reality. This place of open positive expectation is a powerful state of being that keeps you in alignment with your life-stream, allowing for a swift manifestation of solutions and desired realities.

In addition, nurturing self-confidence and successes will naturally generate positive expectations. This is the reasoning behind repeatedly teaching your mind that you ALREADY are these things. One way to do this is by becoming consciously aware of anything joyful in life, no matter how trivial it may seem. However small a reward, expectation releases dopamine and energizes you. By consciously noticing those things that bring you happiness, you train your brain to subconsciously begin the search for more. This, in turn, creates new expectations in the subjective mind.

#8: Tip - _Let Go of How Your Desires Will Manifest_

"How" something occurs, and the power of expectations, go hand in hand. The mind can never know why an event happened, just as it cannot know the overall context of how something will occur in the future. It merely seeks out variables and attracts them. When a person sets narrow expectations regarding how a particular outcome should take place, and they see something different happening, it creates the feeling of being let down, or anxiousness, which can completely sabotage what is being created in their favor.

On the other hand, if that person allows themselves to stay in a place of positive expectation, without creating any negative conclusion about the way a particular event should happen, they stay resistance-free and thus allow their subconscious mind to bring forth the reality that's far better than what their mind could anticipate. Sometimes what seems negative to the mind is part of the unfolding process towards a more positive reality. Avoiding negative conclusions, while remaining in a place of positive expectation under all situations, is the most powerful way to allow well-being to constantly flow into your reality.

Being that the mind is a natural problem solver, letting go of how things will come to be often seems counter-intuitive. However, learning to surrender to that process releases any opposition that the mind attempts to create. Realize that your mind doesn't have the capacity to know enough about the myriad of details and complexities of the issue to handle the job, nor is it necessary that it do so.

Additionally, the processes previously offered encourage mentally living in an "as if it's already mine" state. You must feel as though you already have your desire before actually having it. Once this happens, through repetitive process, the "how" becomes irrelevant because the mind believes in the end result of the wish fulfilled. There's no need for the subconscious mind to recall the middle man of "how" it happened because it does not matter at that point. It just "is." This demonstrates the faith required that creates miracles in a person's life.

#9: Tip - *Meditation*

If we can allow our left/logical brain to get out of the way, we create space for the right brains reality to come forward, creating more balance & joy in our awareness and in our life. Right brain is the home of the subconscious mind. Through the use of meditation, we engage the right brain and the left brain moves into a state of rest. The right brain is then allowed to be more prevalent. From this space, if we lay our desires and intentions, we can manifest and create deliberately in a more effective manner. This balances both hemisphere's of the brain and offers more empowerment. In other words, making conscious decisions to work on your manifestations allows room for the subconscious mind to take the directive.

If you are not experienced with mediation, simply sit in a quiet place, close your eyes, and relax your mind and body by taking a few deep, long breaths. Notice that your thoughts randomly drift in, and then allow them to drift away without any emotional attachment. Begin to consciously observe your natural breathing. If you catch your self drifting to your thinking state, gently revert back to focusing on your breathing. Slowly, the amount of thoughts will reduce as your breathing becomes more rhythmic, and your physical body becomes more relaxed. Bring your focused attention to your intention. Whatever you focus on in this state is in a space that will be impressed directly into your subconscious.

Meditation is a form of conscious sleeping. Scientists have found evidence that people who practice meditation are more aware of their unconscious brain activity, leading to a feeling of conscious control over their bodies, as well as their reality. Just as you sleep to gain energy for your daily functioning, meditation assists in gaining creative energy for what you intend to accomplish. It allows a person the ability to consciously tap into the power of their subconscious mind in order to achieve goals, and has been documented to enable people to attain a higher state of consciousness, greater focus, creativity, self-awareness and a more relaxed and peaceful frame of mind.

When a person meditates on a regular basis, the part of the brain that constantly references back to you, your perspective and experiences, and it's strong, tightly held connection to bodily sensation and the fear centers, begins to break down. As this connection withers, there is no longer an assumption that a bodily sensation or momentary feeling of fear means something is wrong, or that the self is the problem. Therefore, the ability to ignore sensations of anxiety is enhanced as you begin to break that connection, leaving a more positive, healthy and rational subconscious mind.

With time and practice, people become calmer, have a greater capacity for empathy and find they tend to respond in a more balanced way to things, people or events in their lives. This type of behavior transmits a frequency that is favorable for producing positive results where desires are concerned. Still, to maintain new neural pathways that develop through mediation, daily practice is important. Keep in mind that there are many meditative techniques available, and each person should find what works best for them.

#10: Tip - *Become a Conscious Receiver*

One of the greatest secrets to getting what you desire is teaching your subconscious mind that you are a receiver of the things you wish for. You must emit the signal that you are worthy of getting everything you want, and then be open to receiving those things. Imagine that your mind has an antenna available to send and capture vibrations in order to deliver your requests to you. Just as a radio receiver uses an antenna to capture radio waves, process the ones

32

that are vibrating at the desired frequency and then delivers the sound through speakers, your mind uses vibrations in a similar way.

If you carry the feelings of being unworthy, not good enough, disconnected and unlovable, this is not your authentic truth. The real truth is that you were born worthy and perfect and there is nothing you have to do, be or have that will take that away from you. Such beliefs are merely old programming.

Interestingly enough, most people are better givers than receivers. This is because giving provides a person great joy, or a reward to the mind. Receiving is an art that takes practice. It requires intimacy and allowance. However, being a good receiver honors the giver by offering them the same reward in return; the pleasure of seeing you receive. There is nothing wrong with receiving; in fact, all of life itself wants to celebrate in the pleasure of seeing us do so. Additionally, the more we can receive, the more we have to give back.

Practice by receiving compliments generously, and without deflecting back to the other person. Say "thank you" and accept being uncomfortable in the beginning. This may be foreign to your mind at first; nonetheless, you will see that after several repetitions, you will be less and less uneasy and more appreciative of the compliments and yourself. This creates a new boundary for your mind to open up to.

Notice when something good happens in your life and extend appreciation. Gratitude is acknowledgement that what is taking place offers you pleasure so that more can be delivered to you. It also displays awareness that you are a recipient of goodness. The more grateful you are for what you already have, the more you will be able to receive. The subconscious mind will diligently search for more of what pleases you based on the feeling states involved. Instead of focusing on what you don't have, be grateful for everything that you do have -- any situations, relationships, objects and, yes, even your challenges. They are helping you to grow and create more of what you desire.

Begin stating "I am worthy" to yourself as many times as you think to do so until it becomes a belief. The more you use this auto-suggestion, the more your subconscious mind will reveal the truth of that statement. Be committed to having your desires, and realize that all of life is here to support you. Most importantly, practice ways of loving yourself, without the need of approval from others. This loving energy naturally attracts more of what you love to you.

Practice, practice, practice….

Altering the subconscious mind for your benefit is a practice, not a philosophy. This is to say, if you truly want change in your life, there is required time and effort to succeed. The subconscious mind is a powerhouse with unlimited capacity and anyone has the choice to reprogram it to work in their favor, or to be a slave to its prior conditioning. By allowing your belief systems to be changed, you open yourself to new experiences and possibilities in your life. This also empowers your intentions to manifest more readily.

Acknowledge that your thoughts and feelings are nothing but pure, intense energy. What you think in your mind, feel in your body, and therefore carry as beliefs, directly influences what you attract. Consequently, we each have the ability to direct positive energy to our mind in order to fashion a life we desire. Every one of us has the option to use this immense mind power to deliver great wealth, desired weight loss, satisfying relationships, a healthy body and fun experiences. People have miraculously recovered from terminal illnesses and manifested tremendous abundance by simply tapping the power of their subconscious minds.

Your conscious mind has the capacity to be the gardener in a mind equipped to grow whatever you plant. Consciously decide what seeds to use, and place those seeds in the garden of your subconscious mind with the following exercises. Gently cover the seeds and water them daily through application. Soon, somewhere under the soil, a wonderful thing begins to happen. The amazing earth of the subjective mind reacts with the seed. With the continued encouragement of the gardener through conscious effort, a seedling will sprout from the soul and reach for the sun. Your subconscious mind is where this miraculous creative action occurs. Nurture it appropriately and all of your desires will flourish.

3

Exercises to Apply to Any Type of Creation Desired

We create our own reality by our thoughts, beliefs, emotions and expectations. So, all we really need to do to get what we want is to believe we are going to get it and expect it to happen. Easier said than done, right?

Many people have difficulty with the law of attraction due to the matter of convincing the mind to believe that it can have what it wants. This causes doubts, which lead to further difficulty in attaining desires. To get past this, the conscious mind must practice being in charge of subconscious reasoning; it must become the master portion of the mind.

For the law of attraction to work, it is your subconscious mind that needs to believe. The reason many people encounter stumbling blocks, and give up way too soon, is because it can be tricky to get your subconscious mind to do what your conscious mind wants it to. All of the meditation, visualization and positive thinking in the world can prove to be fruitless without your subconscious mind being on board with your desires and beliefs.

Let's get started with the ways in which to do this....

#11: *Exercise - Sleep on It*

The first exercise presented is an excellent process to begin training your subconscious mind in subtle ways. Although it will take some dedication, the rewards are very worth the effort. Through triggering your subjective mind in its most impressionable state, you will be able to easily alter the way in which it begins to believe that your "want" is already something you have -- one of the most important ingredients to successful manifestation!

Step 1

Identify what you want. Find a picture of it, or write out your desire as clearly as possible. What you use in the picture is important. For example: If you want a new home, use a picture of the exact home that you would like to create and write the words, "my new home" so you can clearly read it. Take the time to create this photo exactly as you want it be. If you are unable to find precisely what you want, you can use plain white paper with words as an alternative. For example: "I am deciding to have my dream home by March of 2017," or "I decide to have an extra $1000.00 by this weekend in my checking account." Be specific and precise; keep it short and sweet.

Step 2

Place this picture in a prominent place near your bed where you sleep at night -- preferably positioned in an area where you might look at it as soon as your eyes open.

Step 3

Identify the time of night when you are at your deepest sleep. This is the hour during your slumber when you rarely wake up.

Step 4

Set an alarm to wake you up at that time. It is preferable to use something that gently wakes you up, rather than startles you.

Step 5

When your alarm goes off, look at the picture for 5-30 seconds. If your room is dark use a flashlight to illuminate your picture.

Step 6

Go straight back to sleep.

When you wake up from deep sleep your conscious mind is still hazy, whereas your subconscious (which never rests) is fully functioning. There is no better time than this to completely go around any conscious thinking that may get in the way of your desires.

With this exercise, you are bypassing conscious thinking and speaking directly to the subconscious. So, how does this particular exercise put the conscious mind in control? For the reason that it is a conscious decision to speak directly to the subconscious mind in a language it understands.

Tailor this above method to suit your needs, wants and desires.

Helpful hints:

*Start with small things to prove to yourself that you can create with this technique. The more you're able to create what you want, the more your mind will believe in its power to do so. In this way, success will bring more success.

* It helps if you can go back to sleep right after viewing your picture and just before becoming fully awake.

* The maximum time limit of 30 seconds for viewing your picture is very important. Any longer spent looking at the picture may lead to full consciousness, which could potentially get in the way of the process working for you.

* There is no minimum time to view the picture; even a quick glance at it before going straight back to sleep again works perfectly.

* Don't think about or analyze what you are seeing. The subconscious mind will pick up on the details without you having to force it.

*Train yourself to do this exercise for a minimum of 30 consecutive days; longer if necessary. As earlier stated, repetition is crucial to impress the subconscious mind.

*Use one desire at a time. Once the desire is fulfilled, move on to the next.

#12: Exercise - _Sleep on It (2) – Using Your Dreams to Your Advantage_

This exercise requires a little more practice for most; however, the results are well worth it! It can also be a lot of fun once successfully mastered.

The YOU that is in your dreams is the same you that you are right now. (Say that five times fast!) However, that you is generally unaware of the fact that you are dreaming, and therefore is immediately, upon commencement of a dream, actively within that dream. Lack of continuity doesn't seem to be a problem. Your dreams are also very often used as a filtering process by your subconscious mind, which may work something out or throw something out while you are dreaming. Frequently, the events of your day will come into your dream as your subconscious is processing the affairs.

Step 1

Begin to make a habit of doing reality checks throughout your daily life. Use a soft tone (nothing jarring) on your watch or phone to remind you to do these reality checks, preferably every hour or two.

A reality check is simply stopping and becoming aware of what you are doing. Notice the quality of your consciousness. Ask yourself if there has been a consistent flow of consciousness over the past few hours, and/or if what you are doing at that moment is common to your daily life. Bring your attention to whether there is anything unusual happening, or not. You will generally observe that your quality of consciousness is that of your normal waking life, and that everything in your day has continuity. This may seem a little boring to you after a few "reality checks," however there is solid reasoning for this step in the process. Practice this for several days, weeks or as long as needed for step 2 to work for you.

Step 2

Place your watch or phone near you when you go to bed and set your "reality check" tone to take place while asleep. As in the prior exercise, try to identify the time of night when you're least likely to be awake and set the tone for that time. Once the subconscious mind has memorized the pattern of doing reality checks, it will recognize the tone during your sleep and remind you that it's time, once again, to do one. However, this time you will be completing your reality check while dreaming. This allows you to become lucid during your dreaming state and bring your awareness to anything that is happening during that time.

Depending on how well you keep your habit of doing a reality check during the daytime, you will begin to have conscious awareness of being in your dream once this particular tone is issued. For some this takes a week or two, and for others it could be longer. Consistency during your daily routine is imperative for your subconscious to make it an automatic pattern.

Once this happens, you will begin waking up in a wonderful, weightless reality where you can engage with your thoughts in a seemingly physical fashion. You may be prone to play during the first several dreams, which is very normal. It's also very normal to become overexcited during your first few lucid dreams, which may wake you. Don't get frustrated; just remember that it's working! Keep doing your reality checks and resolve to remain calm the next time you become lucid during a dream.

Step 3

After you've become accomplished with having lucid dreams, you can begin to use them for your law of attraction work. This nonphysical reality is nonetheless real, and if you can make a strong impact here you will be able to manifest your desires in your physical life. Just the same as thoughts, you need to put ample energy, emotion, and time into working on your aspirations; however, it's so much easier on the dream plane because being playful is not challenging for most. In the dream state, you have the ability to simply manifest your desires in an instant fashion. You'll quickly realize that you can immediately enjoy driving that car around, taking a tour of your beautiful house or spending a playful day with your new partner.

The longer you invest time and energy into your desire, just as in visualization work, the more energy you are moving toward manifestation. With lucid dreaming, it's simply easier to actually experience your "visualizations" versus imagining them from within the physical. Your subconscious mind experiences this type of creation in a very real manner and will want to create more and more of what it enjoys -- both in dreaming states, as well as in physical reality.

#13: Exercise - _Generate a Belief That Aligns With Your Intention_

When it comes to the movie of our lives, the first place most of us go to change things is right up to the screen. We spend all of our time, money and energy trying to change our experience on the outside, not realizing that the whole thing is being projected from the inside out.

As mentioned, beliefs are an extremely powerful component of the creation process. If the subconscious mind doesn't believe that

44

something is true, it won't search for ways to validate and create it. Instead of trying to align your beliefs with "reality," it's possible to align your beliefs with what you most want to create in your life.

So how do we change our beliefs? Consider these two points:

A) What you believe tends to become true for you. Our mental map actually creates our life as it believes it to be. Since these maps often become self-fulfilling prophecies, we can change our experience of the world (and ultimately the world itself) by changing the way we choose to see it. If you see the world as a friendly place, you'll tend to notice the ways in which things work out for the best. Because you're looking for "friendly" things to happen, you're that much more likely to find them.

B) You can make believe anything. In order to make believe something is true, you simply tell yourself that it's true, collect evidence that supports your story, and then act accordingly. In this way it's possible to make believe absolutely anything.

Step 1

Choose a goal you have for your life.

Step 2

Write out some things that it would be useful to "make believe" about this goal.

For example:

Goal: "To be financially secure."

Make-Believes:

-"There are thousands of ways for me to bring money into my life."

-"I am a magnet for success and financial freedom."

-"The more I am attracted to financial freedom, the more it is attracted to me."

The idea isn't necessarily to find what you currently believe to be true; rather, anything you think would be useful if you *did* believe it.

Step 3

Use your "make-believes" to create actual beliefs in the following ways:

a) Use a physiology of certainty to teach your mind that the "make-believes" are true. Your subconscious mind understands the language of your physical state. Start by telling yourself something that you know is true. For instance, "Today is _____, and my name is _____." Follow this by repeating your new make-believe in exactly the same tone of voice and holding your body in exactly the same way. Repeat this process several times per day.

When you're able to totally match the voice tone and physiology, the "make-believe" will begin to take root in the subconscious mind as an actual belief. At this point, you'll begin to notice that it actually "feels" truer. It may take a few tries (or even many tries -- each person varies); however, with practice and consistency, each new "make-believe" that you want to make into an actual belief becomes easier and easier.

b) Gather evidence that your "make believe" is true. Plug each "make-believe" into the following format as many times as you can:

"I know this is true for me because_____; for example_____."

For instance:

Make-Believe: "There are thousands of ways for me to bring money into my life."

"I know this is true for me because I've been creating money my whole life; for example, there were many times when I didn't know where I would get the money for something I needed and it always showed up on time."

Or....

"I know this is true for me because I see abundance everywhere I go; for example, I keep seeing the exact car I want so I know it will belong to me soon."

By telling yourself that your statements are true, with evidence of why they are true, the subconscious mind can't argue the validity of them. Therefore, the "make-believe" will become an actual belief which the subconscious mind will seek to validate further by creating more things that align with it.

> c) Act as if your make-believe is true. Ask yourself: "If I knew (make-believe), what would I do to get (my goal)?

For instance:

-"If I knew there were thousands of ways for me to bring money into my life, what would I do to become financially secure?"

Or...

-"If I knew that the more I'm attracted to financial freedom the more it's attracted to me, what would I do to become financially secure?"

This style of inquiry opens the mind to seek new answers. Being that the subconscious mind works to solve a problem in the quickest and most efficient manner, it cannot ignore this method of questioning. It will continue to search for an answer (or multiple answers) until it finds it. When your mind presents you with a list of actions to take, choose at least one to complete in the next 24 hours.

This will add weight to the belief, as well as prompt the subconscious mind to continue coming up with ways to solve the question.

#14: *Exercise - <u>Record Your Intentions</u>*

For those who have some technical skill, an easy way to subtly impress the subconscious mind is with recorded intentions. Through this type of subdued use, these plans gently influence this portion of the mind without coercion. This no-pressure tactic of massaging the subconscious doesn't give it the room to refuse to accept what is being faintly filtered in.

Step 1

Use a computer and microphone to record yourself speaking your intentions. Choose your words and intentions carefully, as this is a very powerful method to influence your subconscious. Go back to chapter two and review precision affirmations and auto-suggestion techniques for helpful hints on ways to do this. "I AM" statements that are followed by what you NOW choose to be tend to incite the most profound changes.

Step 2

Save the file as an MP3 and burn it to a CD, or put it on your MP3 player. If you're going to use this on a CD, add the track as many times as you can fit to the allotted space. For MP3 players, use the loop function.

Step 3

During your daily activities, play the intentions as background noise. Louder is not better. In fact, the more faint and indistinct the background noise is, the more it will surpass any mental blocks. If your conscious mind is eagerly listening to the intentions, this could offer a vibration of resistance.

Through playing the recording as background noise, it continuously impresses the intentions into the medium of sound. This means you are creating quite a bit of physical energy and vibration around your intent. When implemented correctly, the outcomes of this maneuver can be very strong.

Helpful Hint: You can also listen to your recorded intentions as you drift off to sleep to impress the subconscious further. Once again, keep the volume low. There is no need to earnestly listen to what is being said. The subconscious mind will automatically absorb the ideas through recognition of the speech patterns being used.

#15: Exercise - *Go On a Complaint Fast*

Complaining is the opposite of creating what you want in your life. When we complain, we're talking about what we "don't" want. As stated earlier in the book, the subconscious mind will generally cancel out the "don't," leaving only the unwanted thing in a person's reality. One exercise you can use to counteract this habit is to go on a "complaint fast." In other words, attempt to go a day, a week or a month deliberately not complaining about anything.

Step 1

Start with the things you say out loud. Any time you notice yourself complaining, or beginning to utter the words of a complaint, stop yourself immediately. Resolve to go one week without complaining. If you complain even once during that week (and you almost certainly will out of habit), start again with day one. This begins to generate a new pattern in the subconscious mind; it literally trains the mind that complaining is unacceptable AND that you no longer focus on unwanted things.

Step 2

Once you've mastered a week of no complaining, challenge yourself with a month of the same. If you slip up, simply realize you've been doing this your whole life and that it takes repetition to create a new habit. Don't punish yourself for noticing your complaints and attempting to correct a lifetime practice; just realize that it requires persistent efforts to change the routine of your mind.

Step 3

When you reach step 3, congratulate yourself! It's not an easy task to train your mind that you won't utter a single complaint in 30 whole days! Now, complete the same process with the thoughts that enter your mind. Simply let these thought complaints enter and then let them float away. Notice them, and let them go. Immediately following your observation of thought complaints, fill your mind with an opposite of the objections you're developing awareness of.

Example:

Complaint Thought: "I can't believe Bob is slacking off on the job again. This makes my work twice as difficult."

New Thought: "I'm so happy Bob is realizing that his efforts help everyone else stay on task. My job feels so much easier now."

This type of focus, even if it doesn't feel true to you in the moment, will drastically alter what you begin to see in your reality. "Complaint fasting" trains the mind that you expect only good things to happen in your life, which will initiate the creation of those exact results.

Helpful Hint: This is not to say that if you order a salad for lunch and get a hamburger instead you shouldn't send it back. It just means not to follow that up with a list of complaints. Send the hypothetical hamburger back joyfully, knowing that you're manifesting what you really want. It may take some time to complete this task, but the change is incredibly worthwhile!

#16: Exercise - <u>*Create an Intention Symbol*</u>

An intention symbol is created from a statement of your intent. It is a small, often strange-looking symbol that is made by merging several letters together. They are one of the most powerful tools you can use, as they work on so many levels. These symbols are perfect for subconscious mind triggering, as well as altering an immediate (and desired) change within your vibration.

Step 1

Begin by writing down a statement of intent. Your statement may represent material objects such as homes and vehicles, or more permanent desires such as freedom, happiness and love. For instance, "I am attracting love into my life right now." Or, "I have my dream job."

Step 2

Remove all of the power words from your intention; these are the key words in the phrase. For instance, "I am attracting love into my life right now" becomes "attracting love now," and "I have my dream job" becomes "have dream job."

Step 3

Use the first consonant from each word to create your symbol. For instance, "attracting love now" becomes "tln" and "have dream job" becomes "hdj." Once you have your final letters, you are ready to create your intention symbol. This is the part where you can let your creative juices flow. Put all of the letters together in the neatest, tightest way you can. For example:

"tln"   "hdj"

The simpler the symbol is to draw, the better. If you can trace it in about a second, that's best. This way you can produce it anytime you like without having to think about it.

Step 4

Place your intention symbols in places you'll notice it. For instance, you can tape one to your refrigerator, or hang one from the rearview mirror of your car. Or, if you catch yourself doodling, this is a great time to put your artistry to work.

The big trick to these symbols is that your subconscious knows what the intent is behind them. Slightly glancing at these intention symbols throughout the day sends a strong message to your subconscious mind without your having to put any effort into thinking about your desire. This creates the powerful duality of attachment and detachment of your wants at exactly the same time. The more you notice these symbols, the more energy you are putting into your manifestation. Even if you stop consciously noticing them, the subconscious is still seeing them and they are being reinforced.

#17: Exercise - <u>Give the Universe a Task List</u>

This exercise helps you become clear on what you want, while demonstrating faith that the Universe can handle any details you're unsure of. By taking the pressure off of yourself to deal with the things you're uncertain of, you train your subconscious mind to let go of the control it tries to have to fix things that may feel to be out of your realm of understanding. This releases any resistance that creates the opposite results of what you're trying to create. Through using this exercise, you may be amazed at how the Universe will work out the details for you without any more effort on your part.

Step 1

Draw a column down the center of a piece of paper. On the top of the left column, write the words: "Things I'm inspired to do today." On the top of the right column, right the words: "Things I want the Universe to take care of for me."

Step 2

In the left column, write only the things you feel inspired to take immediate action on; the tasks that feel right and clear to you in the moment. Examples might be, "Meditate for 20 minutes," "Have lunch with my best friend" or "Increase my work performance and smile at everyone I see today."

In the right column, write the things that you aren't clear on in the moment. List anything you may feel resistance towards and/or things you aren't even certain how to start yet. Examples might be, "Find an easy and fun way to come up with the car payment," "Send me information to get clear on the next step I need to take for the job I really want" or "Find the right person to fix the plumbing."

Example:

Things I'm Inspired To do Today	Things I Want the Universe to take care of for me
Meditate for 20 minutes.	Find a fun, delightful way to come up with the car payment
Have lunch with my best friend.	Send me information to get clear on the next step I need to take for the job I really want.
Increase my work performance & smile at everyone today.	Find the right person to fix the plumbing.

Step 3

Concentrate only on the left column and leave the right column to the Universe to handle for you.

Any time the Universe accomplishes one of these tasks for you, it's very important to acknowledge its completion and be thankful for it. All of life wants to please you, but it must understand WHAT pleases you first. This also directs the subconscious mind into an understanding that good things just happen for you.

#18: Exercise - *Seeing the World with Fresh Eyes*

Seeing the world with fresh eyes opens the mind to possibilities it may have forgotten about during its normal routine. This prompts it to start to see things differently, and to begin a search of more exciting things in its environment. Through doing this, new circumstances can be created because of the positive expectations that become engrained within the subconscious.

Step 1

Imagine that you have just landed on Earth. Today is your first day here and everything is fresh and new to you. You have no preconceived notions about anything. Immediately, you realize all of the unbelievable experiences you can have on this planet. You take it all in with amazement.

Step 2

Imagine you are writing a letter to someone "back home." Tell them about the residence you're inhabiting and all of the wonderful amenities it has to offer. Emphasize the convenience of such things as cell phones, computers, televisions and cars. Explain the hundreds of food choices you have within minutes of where you're staying. Tell them about people, and how there are so many of them that you can meet and share experiences with. Explain how these people have literally millions of different ways to make money. Talk about all of the options of fun things to do and places to go.

Step 3

For the next few days, keep acting like everything you see is brand new. Get excited about all of the positive things you see around you. Notice all of the wonderful details that you may have dismissed before.

Our brains automatically search for patterns. Through this type of conditioning, new patterns develop that attract new circumstances and encounters. This exercise also produces the feelings associated with wonderment and excitement, which carry a very specific vibratory rate. That vibration attracts the vibration of more excitement and wonderment into your life through fresh experiences.

#19: Exercise - *The "Remember When" Game*

This technique is perfect to swiftly shift your mindset into a new place. As previously stated, the subconscious mind doesn't know the difference between something real and something imagined. Through tricking your brain with this exercise, it recalls an imagined circumstance as something that has already occurred. This creates it as a solid fact, or a belief in the actuality of it.

Step 1

Choose something you'd like to change about your life.

Step 2

Begin to visualize your life with this change in the NOW. Take the time to put yourself directly into the scene of this new creation. Gather all of the feeling sensations you can to match the reality of your new change.

Step 3

Once you've accomplished this, imagine that you are talking with a friend. Tell this friend how you remember the way your life used to be before this change. Recall it as something from the past. Ask your friend if they "remember when" (fill in the blank).

Example: "Do you remember when I used to live in that old apartment building? I remember living there before moving into my beautiful new house. Maybe I'll drive by that old apartment building one of these days just to see what it looks like now. I love my new home and neighborhood so much. I almost can't believe I used to live in that apartment. My life has changed so much since then."

By looking at a current situation as something that happened in the past, you tell your mind that you have moved on to better things. The more you practice this exercise, the more your mind will understand the change as fact and go to work to create it for you. If the subconscious establishes a belief that something has already happened, (in this case, a new reality of your choosing) it will quickly attempt to validate it as true. In other words, it will manifest

60

the details that match it in order to provide evidence to support the event as something that previously occurred.

#20: Exercise - _Make a Shopping List_

When we focus intently on waiting for something to show up in our life, we offer a vibration of worry or lack that creates resistance towards it. This simple process has the ability to take a determined stance regarding the creation of something and turn it into a more flexible desire without conditions attached. Consequently, any vibrations we may carry that prevent our desires from manifesting can be easily released.

This exercise works best with desires that we don't have an extreme attachment to. However, through practicing in this style, and therefore manifesting with great accuracy, we train the subconscious mind that our bigger desires have the ability to come into our life as well. This is to say, belief in your ability to create what you want time and time again generates even bigger beliefs in your ability to create... and so on, and so on.

Step 1

Every day, no matter where you go, scribble out lists of things you see that you want. It's best to write these lists on loose scraps of paper that are unimportant to you; the more lists you create, the better.

Step 2

Treat the Universe like your personal supermarket where nothing is off limits. Pick anything you want, especially luxuries that you'd like to have one day but that aren't at the top of your things to go out and get. Examples: A large flat screen television, new outdoor furniture, a mink coat, etc. Start with anything that you don't have a great attachment to in order to begin seeing magical results.

Step 3

The more you lose and forget about these lists, the easier it becomes for them to manifest. Lists are easy to forget because they're not generally too much we want to think about. (That's why we write them down in the first place.) And in this case, it releases our dreams to the Universe, taking all of the pressure off of the manifestation process.

Helpful Hint: Write a time frame next to the items on your list. For example: A mink coat within the next month; or, outdoor furniture by March. These details help the energy around you understand more specifically what your desire is.

#21: *Exercise - <u>Getting in Charge of Your Vibration with Intentions</u>*

In order to send out vibrations that match your intentions, your subconscious mind must believe in your power to create those intentions. A very simple and influential way to train your subconscious mind is by starting with small intentions that you act on. Through conscious awareness of your intentions, and demonstrating them with ease, your mind begins to place implicit trust on your ability to manifest.

Step 1

Use your everyday tasks and actions to instruct your subconscious mind that whatever you intend will be followed through on. For example, say to yourself: "I am going to walk to the sink and wash this cup." Or, "I am going to write down 10 things I'm grateful for."

Step 2

Create the action that corresponds to your decided intention. In other words, walk to the sink and wash the cup; or, write down the 10 things you're grateful for. Follow through with your intentions as effortlessly as possible. Do it with a smile on your face, feeling how light and easy it is. Throughout the day, announce all small intentions and act them out.

This exercise trains your mind that whatever you intend, and announce, will manifest. Acting out your intentions joyfully and effortlessly teaches the subconscious mind that the creation process is easy and delightful for you. Action is intention made manifest. As this becomes practice, work your way up the scale of things you intend to have happen in your life.

#22: Exercise - *Create What You Already Have*

Teaching your subconscious mind that you are consciously aware of your ability to create what you want is a great way to reinforce the bigger creations you would like to see show up in your life. This type of reminder sends signals to the subconscious mind that strengthen its belief in your aptitude. And because your beliefs are so powerful in what you create, this begins a cycle of more precise manifestations.

Step 1

Look at something you currently have. Announce to yourself, "I have this (fill in the blank)." Examples: "I have this really comfortable bed," "I have a great group of friends" or "I have this ten dollar bill."

Step 2

Recall the day you received this "something." How did you get it? How long did you want it? Did it come to you expectedly, or unexpectedly? Concentrate on the details of what you like about this item and how it serves to make your life better. Does it offer convenience or comfort to you in some way?

Step 3

After concentrating on what is so great about this item, remind yourself that you have created everything in your life. You have already manifested so many of your desires and needs. If you weren't proficient at creating, you would be completely bare of anything in life.

Step 4

Follow that with announcing how powerful of a Creator you are. Repeat to yourself, "I AM a Powerful Creator that can create whatever I choose. I have manifested many things in my life and I am currently manifesting many more things that I desire."

Through focusing your creative intent on what you've already manifested, you can easily remind yourself of the power you possess. Acknowledging your natural competency regarding the creation process attaches additional support to enhance your beliefs systems. Offer gratitude for your creations and be delighted that all of life supports you in your creations.

#23: Exercise - *Become Your Favorite Person*

It's been noted that many people who are prominent in their field spent years examining ways to duplicate the exact formula of those they admire before acquiring their own success. They studied their actions, demeanor, lifestyle, belief systems and anything else they could in order to be able to create an equivalent state of being.

For example, there are many famous actors who have come forward to say that they repeatedly stepped into the shoes of their favorite actor or actress and "became them" as often as possible prior to their own notoriety. This undoubtedly created the necessary subconscious alignment required to be as successful as the person they pretended (and convinced their mind) that they were.

Step 1

Choose your favorite person with regard to how you would like to live your life. This could be a business person, actor, mentor, fictional character or anyone else that you look at and think, "I'd like to live the way that person is living."

Step 2

Think of all of the qualities in this person that you respect and appreciate. What is it about them that excites you? How do they live? What type of partner do they have? What field of work are they in? What physical attributes would you like to duplicate? What do they do for fun? What do you imagine their bank account to look like? What do you value most about them? Or, choose any other characteristics that you notably regard as something that you'd like to have in your life. If there is an aspect to this person that you don't wish to duplicate, leave that off the list.

Step 3

Take all of those great qualities that you find commendable in this individual and begin to imagine that you ARE them, possessing all of those features. Repeat to yourself, "I AM (name of person you admire)" repeatedly. You can follow this statement with, "I have a (fill in the features you like)." Visualize that you are walking around as this person with the life that they have. Experience all of the things you imagine they experience on a daily basis. Think about where they reside and the types of encounters they enjoy. Concentrate on how they behave, what their posture looks like, how they speak and where they spend their time.

Pretending to be the person you admire most in life is a very powerful way to walk in the shoes of what you determine as greatness. This doesn't mean that you want to be that exact person; it merely means that you want to live a life similar to theirs. This exercise is intended to help you duplicate the state of being that you desire in your life. By "becoming" this person, your mind is able to create the feeling states required to manifest that state of being.

If this exercise feels awkward to you, you can leave out the person's name and simply use the attributes you like. Or, you could choose to be great friends with this person instead, knowing they would only develop strong friendships with individuals equal to their character.

Helpful Hint: As you go to sleep at night, repeat the "I AM (name of person you admire)" while thinking of all of the qualities that you chose for yourself until you drift off to sleep. This assists the subconscious mind in its efforts to duplicate and validate these attributes in your life.

#24: Exercise - *Write a Letter Congratulating Yourself*

When we speak to our subconscious mind about something as if it has already happened, it has no reason to argue back about the soundness of it. It sees the imagined scenario as a circumstance that is real. In addition, the more details and feeling states we are able to provide about this "something," the more weight we add to the fact that it has already happened.

Still further, writing this summary on a piece of paper attaches a physical component that gives it a quality of being even more factually valid. With this type of action, the mind is searching for the details in order to put the story into a more solid framework. Once this happens, it becomes a more acceptable account to the subconscious mind.

68

Step 1

Imagine that your life is now full of all of the wonderful manifestations that you set intentions for (or, you can choose to focus exclusively on one particular manifestation). Imagine the new situation you are in and all of the improvements and progress you have made. Visualize how delightful your life has become by being surrounded by your desire(s).

Step 2

Write a letter to yourself describing what has happened. While writing this letter, focus solely on the positive changes that have occurred because of this/these creation(s). Describe the actions you have taken to progress your situation and to create a new quality of life. Recall the benefits this has brought to you and vividly explain them.

In the letter, be sure to comment not just on your practical circumstances, but on your feelings, behavior and actions in the new world in which you are living. How do you look? Act? Feel? Where do you spend your time? What does your typical day look like?

Write down how your needs and values are now being met, and any positive changes to other areas of your life. If there were parts of your life that were not your primary focus, but these areas have benefited as a result of the changes you have made, be sure to note them. For example, you may have changed your career and found that feeling more relaxed has had a positive effect on your relationships.

Step 3

Congratulate yourself for all of these wonderful things. These are your accomplishments and they have been created by you. Write down how good it feels to know that you've skillfully mastered obtaining what you want in life. Describe the pleasure and excitement that you've discovered in your capabilities. Praise yourself for your performance, and for the attainment of your new ability to be successful in all of your endeavors. Use your written words to portray the most vivid depiction you are able to communicate regarding these wondrous feelings. And as you write, immerse yourself in that state of being.

Step 4

Seal this letter and place it in an envelope. Put a stamp on it and address it to yourself. Drop it somewhere to be mailed to you and forget about it until it shows up.

Step 5

When you receive the letter, read your words and recall the accomplishments you've made in your life. Pull up the feelings associated with the words you've written. Remember what it was like to achieve the results you desired for your life. Surround yourself with the feelings of success and stay in that state for several minutes. Read the letter often to produce the sensations that accompany attainment of your goals.

Writing a detailed recollection of an event, and the attached feeling states regarding that event, causes the mind to rush with ways in which to put the pieces of that puzzle together. Reading the letter frequently, while returning to the feeling states that correspond, further impresses this action in the mind.

When the mind has formed a question around a certain event or condition, it must work to make sense of it and form logical reasoning to attach to it. In order to piece this puzzle together, it will create the circumstances that correspond to it so that it may move on to other things.

Helpful Hint: If you find it silly to mail it to yourself, simply place the letter somewhere where you can read it often. You can also incorporate this exercise with the "remember when" exercise by recalling an earlier time when you wrote this to yourself. This will add an additional layer of solidity to it.

For example: When you begin to read the letter you can think or say to yourself, "I remember when I wrote this letter about my accomplishments and how great it felt. It seems like it's been so long since I achieved all of these great things, but it still feels great!" The mind will search for ways to put something that it remembers as a past experience into place.

#25: Exercise - _Subliminal Intentions_

The key to this exercise is using an involuntary action as a trigger for your desires. Because these involuntary actions are so frequent and occur naturally through subconscious commands, this exercise is extremely powerful once established as an automatic behavior by this portion of the mind.

Just as your subconscious mind works the involuntary organs of your body without needing your conscious direction, you can impress it to work other areas of your life by combining directives with these involuntary actions. And as the psycho-physical unit you are (that is, the mind affects the body and the body affects the mind), the subconscious will make this connection through practice and run your chosen affirmations on auto-pilot without any additional conscious effort on your part.

Step 1

To set subliminal intentions into motion, program the following affirmations into your mind each day through repetition. You can do this while in a light state of meditation, or write these down on a note card and read them to yourself whenever you have a break during your day. If the following statements do not apply to the area of your life that you're working to expand, place the words that best suit you into the ending portion of the affirmation for the chosen effect.

Step 2

Affirmations:

"With every breath I breathe each day of my life, my subconscious mind accepts a visual picture of me experiencing a loving relationship (alternatives: a prosperous lifestyle, perfect health, a fun career)."

"With my every heartbeat, each day of my life, my subconscious mind attracts my perfect partner to me (alternatives: more money to me, a fit and healthy body, the perfect job)."

"With every action of my involuntary organs, my subconscious mind accepts a visual picture of me as a person that is worthy of having love in my life (alternatives: more money, outstanding well-being, a creative job that I love)."

Step 3

Add voluntary actions that you take each day to the affirmations in order for your nervous system to be incorporated into the process. This adds great weight to the suggestion inasmuch that the body movement will be recognized as a trigger by the subconscious mind. Try something like the following:

"With every step that I take, each day of my life, my subconscious mind accepts that I am moving towards the greatest love of my life (alternatives: financial freedom, complete healing, an exceptional position at the company I love)."

"With every word that I speak, each day of my life, my subconscious mind sends out vibrations of true love through those words (alternatives: prosperity and wealth, perfect health, a joyful profession)."

"With every blink of my eyes, each day of my life, my subconscious mind visualizes & accepts my new life with the perfect person for me (alternatives: ultimate wealth and financial freedom, a flawless body, the ideal occupation)."

"With every song that I hear, each day of my life, my subconscious mind produces intense feelings of love & excitement (alternative: comfort and security, wellness and physical ease, elation and pleasure)."

Step 4

Once it becomes automatic for you to say these things to yourself throughout your day, it is suggested that you incorporate what is considered to be your three minds (conscious mind, subconscious mind and super-conscious mind) into accepting these new thoughts. You can substitute super-conscious mind with universal mind, higher mind or anything else that resonates with you.

Although changing the subconscious patterns of your mind is imperative and most important to begin with, this visualization triples the powerful effect of how quickly you (conscious), your subconscious (influencer) and the super-conscious (universe) view your reality. This enhances the impression and the quickness of the effect that will take place for you.

For example:

"With every breath I breathe each day of my life, my subconscious mind, conscious mind and super-conscious mind all accept a visual picture of me experiencing a loving relationship (alternatives: a prosperous lifestyle, perfect health, a fun career)."

"With my every heartbeat, each day of my life, my subconscious mind, conscious mind and super-conscious mind all attract my perfect partner to me (alternatives: more money to me, a fit and healthy body, the perfect job)."

"With every action of my involuntary organs, my subconscious mind, conscious mind and super-conscious mind all accept a visual picture of me as a person that is worthy of having love in my life (alternatives: more money, outstanding well-being, a creative job that I love)."

Step 5

Once again, to increase this visualization process substantially, incorporate your nervous system by adding a voluntary action to the suggestions you are giving yourself.

"With every step that I take, each day of my life, my subconscious mind, conscious mind and super-conscious mind all accept that I am moving towards the greatest love of my life (alternatives: financial freedom, complete healing, an exceptional position at the company I love)."

"With every word that I speak, each day of my life, my subconscious mind, conscious mind and super-conscious mind all send out vibrations of true love through those words (alternatives: prosperity and wealth, perfect health, a joyful profession)."

"With every blink of my eyes, each day of my life, my subconscious mind, conscious mind and super-conscious mind all visualize & accept my new life with the perfect person for me (alternatives: ultimate wealth and financial freedom, a flawless body, the ideal occupation)."

"With every song that I hear, each day of my life, my subconscious mind, conscious mind and super-conscious mind all incorporate intense feelings of love & excitement (alternative: comfort and security, wellness and physical ease, elation and pleasure)."

Helpful Hint: The more you incorporate these statements into your daily routine, the more they will become automatic. However, don't make a job out of it or you may introduce resistance that will interfere with the intention of the exercise. Simply begin a practice of reading or meditating on your affirmations several times a day. Early in the morning and before sleeping are highly suggested. Two to five times per day is sufficient, with a minimum of 30 days of application. If it at any point it feels like a chore, come back to it when you are feeling more positive about it.

#26: Exercise - *Create It So*

One powerful way to attract and create your desires is by getting into an optimal state before beginning any manifestation process. Once in this state, your mind is fertile ground to grow whatever you plant. At this point, incorporating feelings states, belief, appreciation and allowance becomes a formula for absolute success regarding intentional creation.

Step 1

Find a quiet room and get into a comfortable position.

Step 2

Think of something that brings you strong positive emotions of love, joy, or gratitude. This can be anything from the birth of a child to a promotion, a new pet, a relationship, etc.

Step 3

Re-live this experience until you can feel the joy in your entire body with all your senses. It is important to feel these sensations in order to get into alignment with the language of the subconscious mind.

As mentioned earlier, emotion and feeling states add great strength to the way in which the subconscious mind responds to your desires. Practice using all, or as many of your senses as possible during this visualization. What did it sound like, smell like, feel like, etc.?

Step 4

When you're in a truly happy state, visualize what you want to create and see it as if it has already happened. For instance, imagine you are driving that new car, living in that new home or enjoying that new relationship. Really get into the feeling and use this experience to its fullest through the use of your senses.

Example: Feel the touch of your fingers on the steering wheel of the car and the pressure of your foot on the gas pedal. See the area you're driving in and visualize the people and other cars around you. Smell the breeze as it comes through your car window and hear the sound of the radio playing. Touch the leather on the seat and concentrate on its texture. Watch the lines on the road whiz by you as you drive.

Step 5

When you've accomplished this sensory rich state, say out loud or write on a piece of paper, "I am so happy and grateful that (fill in the blank). For instance: "I am so happy and grateful that I have enough money to pay for anything I want. And I'm so happy and grateful for this new car experience that I'm having."

Step 6

Write, or say out loud "It is complete; and so it is." Say this in a confident and commanding tone and expect it to happen. This releases your manifestation into the Universe and gives you the freedom to go about your day without any more thoughts that may hinder its progress. With this statement, you are allowing the Universe to handle the portion of creation that you are not equipped to be responsible for.

With the use of this exercise, you incorporate 5 main components to the creation process: Reaching the feeling state of positive emotion, adding a sensory-rich visualization regarding your desire, offering gratitude that the creation is complete, stating it is so as the creator you are and releasing it to the Universe to complete its portion of the process.

This exercise is a very influential effort where the subconscious mind is concerned. It demonstrates power and belief while communicating in a favorable way with respect to the mind's role in the creation process. Additionally, the emotional signature of gratitude means the event has already taken place. Even more so, the latter portion of the process displays faith in the undertaking of your manifestation and allows the subconscious to go to work for you within the limitless realm it occupies.

4

Connecting with the Creative Power of Your Higher Self

When creating your life in an intentional manner, there is no greater power than the connection with the Higher Self. This power has many names, including: God, Source Energy, the Super-Conscious, Infinite Intelligence and the Universe. Whatever you choose to name this power is completely up to you and these processes will work for you when implemented correctly regardless of the name you select. If you do not like the designated titles used in the following exercises, feel free to substitute any terms with ones that resonate with you on a higher level.

These exercises are designed to amplify your creative power through connecting you directly to the powerful energy that you come from. This energy runs through you and has the ability to be tapped in such a way that magnifies your success rate in your daily endeavors and creations. By allowing this creative energy the means to come front-and-center in your manifestation processes, you can intensify any state of being or result you seek in life.

#27: Exercise - _Connecting With Creative Energy_

This exercise provides a connection to pure and intense creative energy. Although this power is always running through each of us, it can become common to forget the potential we possess. Through direct association with the creative energy available, manifestation mastery and speed are dramatically amplified. You can also use this process any time you feel the need to become centered.

Step 1

Close your eyes and take a few deep breaths. Take a moment to concentrate on the fact that you are an Infinite Being in a physical body. Remember that the real you is more than just the material figure you inhabit.

Step 2

Imagine the energy of this Infiniteness within your body as a pure white light. It fills every limb, muscle, cell and fiber of your being as an intense creative energy. Feel it envelope you, knowing it gently provides awareness, safety and security.

Step 3

Visualize this energy beginning to expand out past your physical body. Imagine that it expands out into the room you're in and then it fills the entire building you're occupying. Use your will to expand this energy out even further into the city, town or region you inhabit.

Now, allow this energy to expand out past the country you live in and even further out past the planet. Expand it out beyond all of the other planets, the sun and the moon. Keep visualizing your energy expanding out deep into the Universe until you connect with the light that matches it. If you're unable to imagine this space as light, allow your energy to keep going until you feel a peacefulness resonating through you.

Step 4

In this space, you can manifest anything. This is your pure essence and the creative energy that you come from and are made of. Think of something that you want to show up in your life and how it makes you feel to have it. Begin to possess the feeling states of having this thing in your life and how much it enhances your physical existence.

Step 5

Say to yourself, "I'm so grateful and thankful that this showed up in my life," as if it's already yours. Then say to yourself, "I'm so grateful and thankful that this shows up in my life NOW." Follow that by saying, "I'm so grateful and thankful that I have all my needs fulfilled; and I'm so grateful and thankful that I experience joy in this moment. I'm so grateful and thankful that all the answers that I wanted answered before I came here are answered. I just come to this space and the answers come to me. And I am so grateful and thankful for me being me. And I'm so grateful and thankful for all the good that's coming into my life."

Step 6

Sit in the space quietly and continue to be appreciative of anything that you are grateful to have. Offer appreciation for all of the things that you can think of that improve the quality of your life. Once you've completed this, you can slowly draw your energy back into your body, take a few deep breaths and go back to your daily routine, knowing that you have just created your desires with the whole intensity of the creative energy of the Universe.

#28: Exercise - <u>Who You Really Are</u>

This exercise is designed to remind you of who you really are. It's a way to connect with your Higher Self and to recall the loving, peaceful being that is authentically YOU. This process often has everlasting effects, as it removes the false identity of being less than the magnificent creator you are. In addition, this is a great process for removing any negative or worry thoughts that may be in the way of manifesting what you truly desire.

Step 1

Close your eyes and imagine the higher, spiritual part of you takes one giant step backwards out of your body & rises about two feet above you. Envision that this loving being smiles down at the top of your head and puts their hands on your shoulders.

This Higher Self has been with you since the beginning of time. It absolutely loves you unconditionally and is never angry with you. It never criticizes you, and It understands every decision you have every made and the reason why you made it. This Infinite part of you laughs at the funny things you do, and smiles in loving encouragement as you move through your daily practices. It has no doubts in your ability to find all solutions as soon as you look in the right direction.

This Higher Being is All That Is. While you may sometimes forget your connection to Divineness, It never does. It knows everything you have ever encountered, and It sees the overall picture. While your ego self might not know why you were supposed to meet a particular person today, or be in a certain place at a certain time, this Higher Self knows exactly why. It knows the exact sequence of events that are going to stem from your experiences and the ways in which those experiences have the ability to bring you more of what you want.

There is nothing for you to ever have to do or say to earn its love and guidance. This Higher Self is there unconditionally and always will be. It sees you for the perfection that you are and can be called on at any time to help remind you of it. It has a greater love for you than any human on this planet is capable of; bigger than any parent, child, spouse or partner can give you all combined. You are never alone in this world and will never lack the feeling of being loved when remembering that this Self is always with you.

Step 2

Now imagine that this Higher Self gives your shoulders a gentle,
loving squeeze before stepping back down into your body. This is a
reminder that It is always with you, and always within you. It is not
in the heavens above you out of reach -- nor ever outside of you --
but within you always.

Step 3

Now that your Higher Self is back inside your body, release any
other thoughts that might be running through your head and focus on
this Infinite love. Imagine that this same Higher Self that was
behind you a moment ago is now in the back of your head. You may
even be able to feel a tingle when you think about It. It is still
smiling, still loving; always peaceful and calm. You might start to
feel the tingle run down the back of your neck or your back as you
acknowledge this awesome, spiritual presence. This is you – your
True, Authentic Self.

Step 4

Try this exercise a few times a day when first discovering it.
Eventually you will not need to imagine your Higher Self stepping in
and out of your physical body; you will just feel the tingle and
remember this quite naturally. Eliminate all thoughts if possible and
just focus on this loving, all-knowing Being back there affectionately
supporting you in your endeavors. Silently listen to anything it

might tell you. Know it will happily answer all of your questions if you gently brush your daily thoughts away and give it silent space to come in.

Remember that this Self always sees the bigger picture. It is never worried about little things like bills, work or troubled relationships. Your Higher Self is so big and so knowing that those things are nothing but a tiny speck in comparison to how big you really are. This is the part of you that is always peaceful, and when you focus on it you can feel the peace that envelops your entire being and drowns out anything that may have been worrying you.

After a while, you will find that you can call on this feeling at will. With practice, the moment any tensions might arise you will learn to automatically go to the back of your head and feel the deep peaceful feeling inside so you too can recall the bigger picture.

#29: Exercise - *Creating an Energy Circle*

You may already know that "I AM" are the two most powerful words you can use through your thoughts and words. I AM defines who you are to yourself, those around you and the Universe and Nature. Whatever you say about yourself and the circumstances in your life, both internally and outwardly, becomes a vibration that starts a process (or adds to one) that becomes so. This can work against you if you don't realize the power and importance behind it; however, it can work in your favor just as easily.

Think about the things you think or say to yourself or others that parallel the way your life is now. Many people go through life saying or thinking things such as "I am fat" or "I am broke" and that is exactly what they get. The Universe always gives in abundance to each person as it is designed to do based on thoughts, feeling and emotions that cause the creation process; this applies whether it is a good outcome or a bad one. You tell the Universe what you "are" and it delivers.

This exercise will show you how to positively monitor and enforce the things that you want in your life, while causing a shift in the way that you think. In addition, it quickly connects you with the power of manifestation within both the physical and spiritual plane. Simultaneously incorporating these two powers adds a potency to your creations that is often unmatched.

Step 1

For this exercise you will need a circle on the floor in front of you. This can be an imaginary circle, one drawn on a poster board or you can tape one to the floor. If you have carpet, you can simply use your finger to go against the grain to form a circular pattern. Make the circle big enough to stand in when the time comes.

Step 2

Stand outside of the circle and speak the following affirmations that apply to your desired result. Or, you can choose any of your own affirmations to use. Cup your hand up to your mouth about an inch away so that you can feel the warmth of your breath as you do. After speaking each affirmation into your hand, toss your hand towards the energy circle in front of you as if you're throwing your words from your hand into the circle. This creates a hologram of positive energy.

HEALTH:

I AM grateful for how healthy my body is.

I AM experiencing that my body is balanced on all levels.

I AM experiencing that I have a lot of energy.

I AM thin, fit and tone.

I AM perfectly healthy and in shape.

I AM resting well at night and I wake up refreshed and ready for a new day.

I AM experiencing a physical body that is safe and comfortable.

I AM grateful for my clear, youthful skin.

I AM committed to having a healthy body.

I AM experiencing that exercising is a fun part of my day.

HAPPINESS:

I AM peaceful and serene.

I AM creative and powerful.

I AM a positive person.

I AM always in such a good mood.

I AM enjoying this life and the adventure of each day.

I AM creating more experiences that generate joy in my life.

I AM grateful to be alive.

I AM experiencing that everything I do is good enough.

I AM experiencing my life as easy and fun.

I AM experiencing that things always work out for me.

I AM comfortable moving forward with my life.

I AM manifesting and creating my life positively.

I AM realizing that my internal work changes my outer world.

LOVE & RELATIONSHIPS:

I AM attracting people who are safe and respectful.

I AM attracting people who are understanding, compassionate, loving and kind.

I AM attracting the perfect partner for me.

I AM attracting someone who is thoughtful and considerate of me.

I AM attracting someone who is physically appealing to me.

I AM thoughtful and considerate of myself and others.

I AM appreciating myself and others appreciate me.

I AM easily attract like-minded people with whom I love to interact.

I AM sharing myself and my life easily and I AM understood.

I AM experiencing my intimate relationships as blossoming and growing effortlessly.

I AM grateful for the love I receive from my spouse (significant other).

I AM grateful for the love I receive from my children.

I AM grateful for my spiritual connection.

I AM experiencing that my relationships are nurturing, healthy and improve my life daily.

I AM loved and supported.

MONEY:

I AM financially free and secure.

I AM creating large sums of money.

I AM worthy and deserving of the prosperity that is intended for me.

I AM experiencing that money flows easily into my life.

I AM always bringing in money faster than I AM able to send it out.

I AM grateful for the money that is flowing to me from different sources.

I AM experiencing that money comes to me from both known and unknown sources.

I AM comfortable with large sums of money and have fun with it.

I AM generous in sharing my money because I know there is plenty for me and others.

I AM successful and abundant in all ways.

TIME:

I AM experiencing that I have all the time I need each day.

I AM moving between the different activities of my day with ease and grace.

I AM always on time for my commitments.

I AM experiencing that others are always on time for me.

I AM flowing easily within the structure of time in my day.

I AM experiencing that people are considerate of my time.

FOR ALL:

I AM creating more of what I want in my life effortlessly.

I AM assisted by the powers and spirits of the Universe who take care of all of the details of bringing me what I have asked for.

I AM grateful for this powerful assistance.

I AM easily able to manifest my desires.

I AM continuously growing and evolving.

I AM finding life to be supportive and joyful.

I AM attracting good things to me each and every day.

I AM worthy of a life of bliss and happiness.

I AM a powerful creator.

Step 3

Once you have thrown the energy of each of your affirmations into the energy circle, step into it and feel this powerful energy wash over you. Imagine that this energy is flowing all through your body as a brilliant white light. This light energy grounds itself into the earth through your feet and illuminates out and above your crown and into the Universe. In this moment, your desires are rooted in the physical plane of manifestation, as well as soaring with the Universal energy that creates.

Place your hands on your feet and feel this energy rooting itself into the Earth. Gently work your hands up your body all the way to your crown and out above your head with your arms raised. Now, imagine that this energy is being sent into the Universe for its realization and materialization. Stay in this energy circle for as long as it delights you, knowing that both the spiritual and physical energies of creation are working for you and through you.

Step 4

Afterwards, you may choose to say a prayer of gratitude. Give thanks for the wonderful things that are now being put together for you and coming to your life.

This energy circle starts the formation of your affirmations to be manifested into your life. You are telling the Universe what you believe about yourself and what you want to experience in your physical existence. It is recommended that you do this exercise daily and watch the miracle of how quickly your life can change. You may add to or modify the" I AM" affirmations to fit your life more specifically if you so choose.

Helpful Hints: Practice adding affirmations to your energy circle often to increase the creative process. You can also step into this circle any time you wish to feel the energy of it moving through you. This is great reinforcement for the mind and vibrational state.

#30: *Exercise - Assembling a Spiritual Counsel*

In this exercise you will mentally assemble your own Spiritual or Invisible Counsel to provide you with advice and direction when you have a question or difficult decision to make. On a subconscious level, this type of exercise triggers the switch that causes it to seek the answer to any queries it's presented with. On a more spiritual level, you are intermingling with Infinite Intelligence's all-knowing answers to manifest your desires.

Step 1

Write or mentally form a list of questions pertaining to your issue at hand. As stated in an earlier chapter, it's great to formulate some of these questions in the "What if" and "What else might be possible that I haven't considered" styles in order to generate the types of responses you're seeking. However, you can incorporate more direct questions also.

Step 2

Set aside at least 15 minutes to imagine that you have invited specific guests of your choice to a meeting. These guests are hand-picked by you based on their expertise with certain matters. Five to ten guests are generally sufficient, however you can reduce or increase the number as necessary.

These guests can be living or dead, as long as they inspire you on some level. For instance, you may choose Biblical characters and faith-based gurus for spiritual guidance, famous athletes or doctors for advice on health and physical well-being, actors and artists for creative solutions or well-known businessman and wealthy people for money and business concerns.

Step 3

Close your eyes and imagine that you are sitting in a boardroom where there is a large conference table surrounded by empty chairs. You are sitting at the head of this table and waiting for each of "your" counsel members to appear. You can imagine any number of vacant seats around this table, depending on how many guests you've decided to have.

At times you might only want to invite the people who can help with a particular problem. For example, you may invite Bill Gates for a money or business matter that you need assistance with. Or, you may choose to invite multiple characters in order to get each of their unique opinions on a subject. You may even realize that certain personalities that you've chosen for other reasons may elegantly speak up on topics where you would not have expected their advice.

Step 4

Now mentally ask the questions that you've formed and silently wait for each of these people to answer. Pretend as if you are in a real meeting. Do not be discouraged if some of your guests do not respond at all. Also, note that not every answer may be a verbal response. They may also come in the form of a gesture, a mental picture or a telepathic response.

Take notes as you would in a real meeting, and don't dismiss any answers given to you. Pay attention to the distinct responses you receive, and give yourself some time to get used to the possibility of any unusual ideas if they feel a little uncomfortable. Most importantly, be open to the fact that any/all of the replies have the potential to move you into a solution.

For example:

Let's say you have two credit card bills and you are wondering which one you should pay off first. Your first natural instinct might be to pay off the creditor who is yelling the loudest, but you're not certain if this is the best route to take. From your boardroom chair, ask an investment guru of your choice if this is the correct action. His advice might be, "Pay off the one with the highest interest rate so it will cost you less in the long run." Or, "I wouldn't pay either of them until calling both companies and negotiating a better deal with each."

With this exercise, and the types of questions you pose, your subconscious mind and spiritual connection are able to offer you direction that may otherwise never enter your habitual mind. This practice allows you to open yourself to any unique answers from your Higher Self and the hidden recesses of your mind power. Sometimes we get so used to hearing our own mental voice with its customary way of thinking that we forget we are actually allowed to think outside of our own box. You may find that the best part of this exercise is that the suggestions given actually work.

5

Manifesting Money Exercises

Our minds and emotional states are designed to stay in repetitive patterns, whether advantageous, or not. The thoughts we think are the electrical charge in the quantum field, and the feelings are the magnetic charge in this field. How you think and feel about any particular subject influences every atom in your life; therefore, these two things affect every outer condition.

Through adjusting your energy to align with states of abundance, you can easily alter the course of your outer financial conditions. In other words, elevated thoughts and emotional states bring elevated results. Try the following exercises to increase your abundance manifestation power.

#31: Exercise - *Anchoring the Vibrations of Abundance*

This exercise will teach your mind and body how to send out vibrations of abundance. In addition, you will learn to create an anchor to instantly access that vibration of abundance any time you wish. By matching the vibrational frequency of abundance and prosperity, you are able to effortlessly attract money into your life.

Simultaneously, this teaches your mind that abundance is a regular occurrence in your reality through the feeling states associated. To perform this exercise, place your logical thinking aside for some time and become totally immersed in the thoughts and feelings of abundance and financial freedom.

Step 1

Take a few deep breaths and begin to take on the assumption that you are a millionaire. Being that you're a millionaire, what is the setting you're in? Who is with you? What are you experiencing? With all of the money that you need to feel secure, what is your life like now? What changes characterize the fact that you are now rich?

Step 2

Further impress your mind and body with being a millionaire. Now that you're totally secure in your finances, ask yourself the following questions: What types of thoughts are you free to entertain that you didn't delight in before? What types of decisions are you able to make about your life that are different now that you have money? What types of actions can you take now that you're free to do as you please?

Step 3

Imagine that you're out shopping just for fun. Adjust your body language to that of a rich person; someone who can freely go out and spend whatever they please. Think about the confident state that goes with this type of financial freedom. Anything you want to have can be yours. How are you holding your head now that you're financially secure? What position are your shoulders in? How straight is your back? What look is on your face? What feeling and sensations do you have in your body?

Look at the things you want to buy and realize that you can have any, or all of them. What do you want to buy for yourself? What do you want to buy for your friends and family? What would you like to buy for your new estate? What types of toys do you want to play with?

Imagine how poised you are when the salesman asks if he can assist you. This is different than before. This time you can choose any style, any add-ons, any additional accessories and any price tag. You are absorbed in the feeling of being able to be as free as you want where spending money is concerned. Capture those feelings and hold them as long as you're able to. In your mind, point to anything you wish and confidently say, "I'll take one of those, and one of those and one of those!" Let yourself be immersed with how good it feels to have whatever you want.

Step 4

Once you have a solid feeling of abundance, notice how it moves through your body and gets stronger and stronger. As you concentrate on this building feeling, use your dominant hand to lightly pinch the crease between the thumb and index finger of your

101

non-dominant hand. Apply gentle pressure to this area while you continue to feel this feeling increasing; enough pressure to feel that you are doing this, but not so much that you experience discomfort. Keep doing this until you have the strongest feeling of abundance you can develop. While at the peak of this feeling state release the pressure from this area and take a few deep breaths.

Step 5

Test your abundance anchor. Pinch the crease in your hand in the same manner you did before. What happens? If you've impressed the subconscious mind sufficiently with the feelings of abundance, you should notice those feelings increasing once again. If you aren't able to re-access the abundance state, then start the process again. Repeat the exercise once or twice a day until you are able to reproduce the feelings with just the use of your hands. When the anchor is successfully created, you'll know it!

Step 6

Once you've accomplished setting your abundance anchor, take moments to apply gentle pressure to your hand in the same manner as before during your daily routine. Once every hour or two is enough – remember to try not to force results. Every time you re-access these feeling states with your abundance anchor, you powerfully send out the vibration that correlates with prosperity and abundance.

For increased results, it's suggested to use this exercise for a minimum of 30 days in order to develop a habit that is recognized by the subconscious mind that will begin producing results. In doing so, you'll be matching the vibrational frequency of abundance that will attract it into your life. Simultaneously, you're teaching your mind that abundance is a regular occurrence in your reality. Being that your subconscious speaks the language of feelings most dominantly when creating and validating your life, this is an extremely effective method to begin manifesting more money. In other words, the mind will feel abundance as your reality and search for ways to prove that it's true.

Helpful Hints: Any time you begin to notice thoughts and feelings of worry and lack it's a great time to use this trigger to reverse the feeling states. Also, this exercise can be used for all types of manifestations; however, it's particularly beneficial when creating money. If you find yourself forgetting to use your abundance anchor, set an alarm on your phone or watch to remind you to use it. Or, you can set a mental reminder that is attached to things you do in your daily routine, such as brushing your teeth, getting into your car or opening the refrigerator door.

#32: *Exercise - Spend a Million Dollars*

This exercise is a 30 day process and well worth the effort. You are going to teach your mind not only that you have plenty of money to spend, but that spending money is really fun. Once again, this helps the brain seek out and attract corresponding circumstances, as well as adjust your vibrational state to one of wealth. You will need a pen and paper (or notebook) for this exercise.

Step 1

Day one: You have to spend one thousand dollars any way you wish. Find an item that you would like to have that has a price tag of no more than a thousand dollars. Grab your pen and paper and write a description of the item in your notebook and paste a picture next to it if possible. List as many details as you can about this item -- the more specific you are, the better. Make a detailed record of how this item makes you feel. It's important to spend as much time on your emotional state when writing as possible. Talk about how it felt to purchase it, and recall your feelings associated with now having it.

Day two: You now have two thousand dollars to spend. Follow the same steps of writing a detailed description and attaching a picture of the item. Once again, make vivid account of your emotional state after the purchase.

Step 2

Repeat this process daily. Increase your budget by a thousand dollars every day until you get to ten thousand dollars ($10,000.00) on day 10.

Step 3

On day 11, begin to increase your budget by ten thousand dollars ($10,000.00) every day until you get to one hundred thousand dollars ($100,000.00) on day 20.

Step 4

On day 21, increase your budget by one hundred thousand dollars ($100,000.00) every day until you get to one million dollars ($1,000,000.00) on day 30.

Be sure to write these details in your notebook daily for the full 30 days of the process. By doing this, you will change your subconscious mind's perception of money. Incrementally, this exercise causes a shift that teaches your mind to focus on how fun it is to have money and spend it. In this way, it will start to feel the fullness of having money and the pleasure of putting it to use while establishing a series of larger and more acceptable boundaries. This changes its outlook to one that will attract more money into your life.

#33: Exercise - <u>Let Money Chase YOU</u>

This visualization turns the tables on the energetic equation between money and those that seek to have more of it in their life. Due to the freedom that the value of money offers, many people will spend a majority of their time "wanting" more of it. This type of energy causes the mind to believe in its unavailability because a "want" is something that we don't actually have; and believing that something is unavailable will produce just that. It causes resistance that holds the object of that "want" away from us.

Once there is the realization that abundance is available for all, there is no longer a need to crave for things desired. Additionally, creating the space for desired things, through the correct energetic application, offers an allowance of those things to show up in daily, physical existence.

Step 1

Imagine that you are sitting in a beautiful field. As an intricate part of Nature, there is nothing about this field that isn't dripping in abundance and large quantities. The hundreds of trees that outline the grass of this field hold thousands and thousands of leaves; there are millions of tiny insects that call this field home and literally billions of blades of grass as far as you can see. As you sit in this field, you are able to realize the abundant manner in which Nature always operates. Take a few moments to relish in the fact that you are also a part of the natural order of things, which clearly makes you an abundant being.

Step 2

Imagine that it begins to lightly rain. Think of the millions and millions of rain drops that are beginning to fall on this field. This is just another example of the way in which Nature is only capable of supplying in an abundant way.

Step 3

As you sit in this field feeling the rain wash over you, begin to notice that this rain doesn't feel wet. This rain feels like paper, or fabric. In fact, this rain (that comes from the abundance of Nature itself) is actually money falling all around you. Feel it fall on your head and your shoulders. Notice that it brushes past your face and that there are stacks of it beginning to accumulate in your lap. Place your hands out to feel the fabric of this money between your fingers. Pull several pieces up to your nose and smell its natural scent. Hear how it sounds as it falls into piles and notice the quantity of money that has gathered around you.

Step 4

Now, as odd as it may sound, you're going to have a conversation with this money. Nature has chosen to abundantly supply you with wealth and financial freedom; it has selected you as the perfect candidate.

The symbolic faces on the money surrounding you begin to ask if it's ok if they can live with you. Nature has told them that you are a good place for them to take up residence, and they each take turns asking if they may. They want to make sure that they are safe, cared for and will be sent out into the world when it's their time to be used in a productive way. And, they have chosen you as the perfect host for this.

As you graciously allow each one of them the opportunity to stay with you, you hear more of them asking, "Can I come too? What about me? May I live with you also?" Take a moment to nurture this money and tell it that you'd be happy to let it to come home with you. Imagine each piece of money's ecstatic response when it hears it has been chosen by you as a new member of your home. It knows that you will care for it and allow it to perform what it's designed to do.

Step 5

Realize how Nature has perfectly married you with this abundance, and be joyful in its flawless decisions. It takes delight in offering grand supply to its entire offspring. Offer gratitude for not only your gift, but for the fact that you are able to be such a good environment for this money to thrive in. Show appreciation for the opportunity to take care of this money in the way it needs to be supported.

With this exercise, money is seeking you, rather than the other way around. You've made yourself a good host; therefore, it desires

YOU. Stop to ponder whether you've ever considered this to be a possibility. If you've endeavored to intentionally create money in your life, ask yourself how much power you give it. The dance of energy between you and financial freedom is delicate due to any subconscious blocks that may be in the way. Once your mind believes that money freely desires to be in your existence, you may find it showing up in ways you never dreamed of.

#34: Exercise - *The Sandbox*

As previously mentioned, we often place great significance on how powerful money is, which increases the amount and type of energy it carries within our own personal realm. However, money is merely a means to new experiences and comforts; it's simply a "middle man" to what we really desire in our life. It's not actually money that we want; rather, it's the experience, security, luxuries and fun that are sought after.

This simple exercise will get you into the abundant feeling necessary to begin calling money into your life, while aligning you with your passion. You must match the experience on an internal level in order to have it attracted to you. Through this process, you learn to bring back the child-like you that believes the sky-is-the-limit without worries, frustrations or annoyances. This state implies implicit trust in the real reason you came into a physical existence to begin with – fun!

Step 1

Begin to visualize your life as one giant playground. This playground is designed in a way to offer you the most fun experience possible. You push all of the "hard stuff" aside and choose your own personal amusement first and foremost. The pleasure you encounter here is your new "job" in life. Realize your amazement and awe to discover how wonderful and entertaining this playground is.

Step 2

Step into the massive sandbox on this playground. In it are all of the parts of your life that you most enjoy. You start to notice how this sandbox is designed just for you, and how pleasing it is to be here. Like a child, it's almost difficult to pick which thing you would like to experience first due to how thrilling everything around you is.

Step 3

Begin to discover what new toys are in the sandbox. What looks to be the most fun to play with? What types of experiences and adventures can you have here? What are your absolute favorite things in this sandbox of life? Do you see any other cool kids that want to play with you and increase your fun factor?

Step 4

Imagine that you're playing "business" with these cool kids. What types of products and services do you want to create for them? What is the most fun business you can play with that makes you happy? Is this a new product or service? Is it one that you've added your own personal touches to? This is YOUR sandbox, so you can make your business ANYTHING you want. The possibilities are unlimited. The ideas are endless.

Step 5

Begin offering these services and/or products to the other kids. Imagine how much it enhances their fun time and how much joy you bring them. See them delighted with what you've offered them and notice how many more kids want some of what you're selling too. Money is a simply byproduct that doesn't carry much thought with it; it's an unintended consequence of the fun, joy and adventure you're experiencing. Stay in this sandbox for as long as you're having fun with your booming business.

Through adopting the perspective that life is meant to express the passion within, and thoroughly enjoying yourself in the process, you are automatically aligned with abundance. When we're serious about our work, we often "work hard." Things don't happen in a natural manner with this type of energy because of the focus on all of the details, rather than joyfully putting them into place.

Incorporating the "law of least effort" seems counter-intuitive on a subconscious level. However, when we're serious about work and money, we worry about finding the ideal solutions rather than allowing them to find us. Trying to force results into place will offer resistance that undermines the goal intended. By taking time to enter our "fun zone," we are a 100% match to the very things we most desire. Consequently, we can easily manifest money because we're open to it. Seriousness will almost always pinch off the flow of prosperity.

#35: Exercise - *Energizing Your Abundance Intentions*

This exercise is an energetic power-punch that has been proven to manifest money very quickly. Although a bit more on the Metaphysical side, it also holds great weight within the mind inasmuch that the body and spirit are working in unison with it towards the intention. This amplifies the process from the psycho-physical unit aspect.

Step 1

(Optional) Clear the space in a room of your home by burning some cleansing incense such as sage, frankincense or sandalwood.

Step 2

(Optional) Safely light four candles in the four corners of your room. These candles serve as the light and as also symbolize that you are pulling metaphysically from all four directions and all four elements: Air, Fire, Water, and Earth.

Step 3

Stand in the center of your space and close your eyes with your arms stretched out and palms facing each other as if holding a ball of light. Visualize this ball of light growing brighter and stronger in between your hands. Imagine that it is pure, positive, creative energy that has come to assist you with your intended manifestation.

Step 4

Begin to fill this ball of light with your abundance intentions. You can use the ones below from #29: Exercise - Creating an Energy Circle, or create ones that best suit you. Mentally project these affirmations into your ball of light, or speak them into your hands for an even deeper impression. Visualize this affirmation light growing in power and intensity. See how almost impossible it is to contain its brightness within your hands. Feel the warmth of it on your palms as you increase its strength with your intentions. Hear the hum of its energetic force as it magnifies and grows even stronger.

Affirmations:

I AM financially free and secure.

I AM creating large sums of money.

I AM worthy and deserving of the prosperity that is intended for me.

I AM experiencing that money flows easily into my life.

I AM always bringing in money faster than I AM able to send it out.

I AM grateful for the money that is flowing to me from different sources.

I AM experiencing that money comes to me from both known and unknown sources.

I AM comfortable with large sums of money and have fun with it.

I AM generous in sharing my money because I know there is plenty for me and others.

I AM successful and abundant in all ways.

Step 5

Once this ball of energetic light has reached its maximum force, gently open your hands and release it (along with your abundance intentions) upward into the Universe. With your eyes still closed, visualize the ball of light flying way up and then exploding in the heavens and causing it to shower gold coins all around you. Feel the

114

money; see the shimmering reflections of the gold; hear the coins clanging together in piles all around you; allow the excitement to fill your body with enthusiasm and eagerness. For a few moments, say to yourself: "Wealth, prosperity, money and abundance constantly flow to me from the Infinite Field of the Universe."

It's suggested to repeat this exercise daily for a minimum of 30 days. Although steps 1 and 2 add more energy to this exercise, they can be eliminated for the sake of time if necessary. This process provides intense results when practiced consistently. It demonstrates faith in the energetic connection that is necessary to create, as well as a sensory-rich experience that the mind will deeply connect and align with.

#36: One money trick:

Teach your mind to believe that money really does grow on trees by repeatedly telling it so. Well, it grows from plants anyway; linen (the flax plant) and cotton to be more precise.

Money itself isn't worth any more than the paper it's printed on. We only give it value based on the equivalence that others have given it. By teaching your mind a new belief through repetition, one that money actually grows from Nature, which is always lavishly abundant, you remove the subconscious block that has the perception

115

of money being a scarce commodity. Nature doesn't have the capacity to produce anything in an inadequate manner.

6

Relationship Exercises

When it comes to the relationships of our lives, many people are either not-so-lucky in love, or they find themselves wishing someone would treat them differently. As the following exercise will reiterate, the only reason we experience these negativities is because we believe on a subconscious level that we still need to experience them, or can't move past them. The following processes will help you knock down the barriers that block you from creating the types of relationships you desire in your life. And if you're looking for the perfect partner, you can attract him or her too!

#37: Exercise - *Changing the Scripts in Your Life*

Our life is full of people who play "roles" for us in our daily interactions. Knowing that you are a creator-being with the abilities of thought and feeling, you most likely have the perception that you have the power to influence changing or leaving people out of your life. Being able to imagine that the people in your "script" who are treating you poorly, as people who are changing to treat you well, is a very strong exercise is causing change in your life.

Believing that you are worthy and deserving of being treated with love, honor and respect is even more powerful. The only reason that these negative experiences occur is because at some level you believe this is how you should be treated. In order to make changes to the types of relationships you experience, your mind must believe in these changes on a core level. Use the following visualization process as often as needed in order to prompt the changes you desire from the people you have in your life.

Step 1

Imagine that your life is a play and that you are standing on a stage with all of the people in you know. Begin to offer gratitude and thank all of the people on your stage for helping you learn your life lessons. Each of them has played their parts very well and should be recognized for the instruction they have offered you.

Step 2

Invite all of the people that have played a part with a negative script to come forward and throw their negative scripts into a large bonfire at the front of the stage. If there are any people that are unwilling to throw their script into the bonfire, simply direct your stagehands to politely escort them off of your stage so they can act out their negative role in someone else's play. This option pushes past any subconscious blocks that may try to stop you from proceeding.

Step 3

Once the old scripts are up in flames, begin to imagine your Higher Self (in any way you choose to visualize that) standing there with a bright light surrounding him or her. Notice how powerful and loving this energy is. Your Higher Self hands out new scripts to everyone, including you. All of these new scripts direct everyone to love and honor you. Your new script reads that you are now ready to receive all of this love and honor because you now love and honor yourself.

Think of everyone with their new scripts and watch as they are reading through them with delight and getting familiar with the details. You can, at this point, show any individual in your play the important aspects of their script that you would like for them to particularly notice so you are assured that they are aware of these changes in their behavior towards you. You may read over certain specifics with them and visualize the words on their scripts that indicate the positive changes. You can also show them your new script where it says that you are loving and honoring yourself, and how grateful you are that you are loving and honoring each other as well.

Give gratitude to each of these individuals for their willingness to play their new role. Everyone is happy to do so, because they know this is your play and they want to show up in it as you have directed them to do. Begin to feel positive about their new roles and announce how excited you are about the new scripts because you know it is for the Higher good of everyone on your stage.

Step 4

Begin to imagine everyone acting out his or her new role. Notice in detail the new healthy and loving behavior you are experiencing in your play. Remember, at any time, you can stop your play and change the scripts as many time as you want to. Imagine that the people in your play are agreeable and willing to take any new directives or alterations you give them. If they are unwilling to take the new script, you may have them escorted off of your stage.

Step 5

Once you're satisfied with the rehearsal, come back to your daily life. Repeat this process once a day until you begin to notice the changes within the people around you. Remember to take your attention away from anything you detect that resembles the old roles these individuals display so you don't nullify any of your desired changes. You can easily do this by realizing that your subconscious mind will catch up to the new alterations once a pattern is established. Consistency is key.

Remember this: The Higher Self of everyone in your life really loves and honors you. The only reason you may not be experiencing this with certain individuals is because you still believe you need people to play roles with negative parts for you. This is merely a pattern that is fixated in the subconscious mind. With practice, this exercise trains the subconscious that this is no longer necessary in your life.

Let all of the "bad guys" in your play become "good guys." You no longer have to keep playing out the drama of hurting, judging and controlling one another. Through utilizing the power of the Higher Self within you in this exercise, you teach your mind that you can draw that same energy out of others in your interactions with them. Consequently, those interactions will change for the better. In fact, after some repetition, you may be amazed to see how these individuals are acting towards you in your physical reality.

Helpful Hint: Each time you complete this exercise, use this affirmation to solidify the results: "I am attracting people into my life who respect, honor and love me; and I respect, honor and love them. My Higher Self brings out the best in all those I meet and interact with. I am grateful for the comfortable and positive interactions that I have daily with all of the like-minded people who are in my life."

#38: Exercise - *Attracting a Partner*

In order to attract the exact type of partner you'd like in your life, specificity is extremely important. This process will help you become clear on precisely the sort of person that you'd like to fill this area in your life. In addition, it assists in the declaration of why it's important to you and the announcement of your power to manifest him or her; all powerful components in the creation process.

Step 1

Divide a piece of paper into three columns; or, you may choose to use three separate pieces of paper. Label your first column "What I Want, your second column "Why I Want This" and your third column "Why I Will Have It."

Step 2

Begin by writing down all of the things you want to have in your perfect mate under the "What I Want" column. What are their physical characteristics? What is their approximate age? What other positive qualities do you appreciate in this person? How does this person make you feel? What types of things does this person do that delights you? What types of things do you do together? What type of lifestyle does this person live? What sorts of non-physical characteristics fit this person's description? Examples: Kind, generous, spiritual, forgiving, loving, affectionate, thoughtful.

Pretend you are placing a special order for this individual to come into your life, being as positive and descriptive as possible. Write until you can't come up with anything else.

Step 3

Write down all of the reasons why you want this person in your life under the "Why I Want This" column. Although it's been said that a "want" is something we don't currently have, this style of questioning gets to the heart of the reasons it would strengthen your life. In other words, it shifts the focus and feeling states from "want" to acknowledgement of formed judgments for having it.

How will having this relationship enhance your life? How will it strengthen you as a person? What level of joy, happiness and/or love do you imagine with this person? How will this relationship build you up? How will it change your current circumstances in a positive way? What does this person add to your life?

For example: "This relationship is so awesome for my life because it lifts me up and motivates me. This partner offers me excitement and encouragement while also loving me in the most intimate ways. I'm a better person for having this partner because I walk around with my head held high and nothing can wipe the smile off of my face."

Step 4

You probably realize by now that you'll be filling in the third column. This "Why I Will Get It" column is very important because you're creating and announcing a firm decision as to why this relationship will be yours. This doesn't leave any room in your mind or the Universe for dispute. It demonstrates clarity and faith.

What lets you know that you will have this relationship? How do you know this is the person for you? What decisions have you made regarding how firm you are about creating the perfect person for you? Why do you deserve to have this partner show up? What's so awesome about you that will make it impossible for this person to be able to resist being magnetized to you? What are your great qualities as partner? What positive things do you come to the table with in a relationship?

For example: "I'm now making the decision that this is the relationship for me. I know exactly what I want, down to the small details, and I intend to have it. I am open to love and ready to share my life. I have so much love to give and I always make sure I'm considerate of my partner's feelings. There are a million other people that might want to have a relationship with me, but this is the person I choose."

Step 5

For one week, resolve to add at least three new responses to each column you've created (more if you think of them). If you are having difficulties adding new things, ask your subconscious mind what other attributes are important to you that you may have dismissed. This will prompt it to search diligently to find the answers for you and help you to become as clear as possible on what it is that you really want in a relationship.

Step 6

Choose a list of strong words from each column and write them on pieces of paper that you can place in different areas of your home, car or work place. For instance, from column one you may choose all of the positive characteristics of the person you're creating. Examples: handsome, tall, generous, adventurous. From column two you may choose power words such as encouragement, motivation, or excitement. And, from column three you may come up with a list of words such as love, considerate, share or relationship. Ten to twelve total words from the three columns is sufficient. This list is a powerful representation of the relationship you will have.

Step 7

Place these power words on pieces of paper and post them in areas where you will see them several times throughout the day. For example: Your bathroom mirror, the refrigerator door, on your car's dashboard, your desk at work or a cell phone list.

Similar to the Creating an Intention Symbol Exercise, you don't need the full list of sentences for your subconscious mind to recall the details. Your mind will recognize the meaning whether you put conscious thought into them, or not. These powerful pieces of paper, with ten or twelve of the words you've chosen regarding your new partner, are ample enough to trigger the emotions that excite you about this person. And, those emotional states make it much easier to attract the person of your dreams.

This exercise creates clarity, precision, reasoning and decisiveness. When we're able to be very specific about our desires, create the feelings associated with them through analytical thinking and broadcast our intent with unwavering sharpness, we send a powerful signal that says, "This is specifically what I want, why I want it and why I'll get it."

Since the Universe responds to our feelings (and therefore our vibrations) the most, duplicating this state multiple times per day through subconscious triggering adds an element that increases your success rate. With those triggers, you are both attached and detached from the outcome simultaneously, which is one of the main ingredients to attracting what you want in your life.

#39: Exercise - *Sexual Transmutation*

Sexual energy is life force energy; it creates new life. When we're not in the place of creating human life, this energy is ideal to be used for other types of creations. Sexual transmutation uses sexual desire to manifest tangible effects in the physical world. One of the most powerful experiences that we have as human beings is the energy of excitement. If we can pair this energy with intent, then we can direct one of the strongest manifesting forces available on earth. And what better way to use this energy than to manifest the perfect partner?

The process of sexual transmutation has been used for thousands of years to create events that seem miraculous. Due to our modern sexual practices and beliefs, it may take some time to get proficient at the method of sexual transmutation. However, you will likely find it a pleasant enough exercise to do every day. Through consistent practice you will get better and better at the process and most likely be amazed at the results.

Step 1

Create a space where you will be undisturbed and come into a state of conscious breathing. Take a few moments to fantasize about a sexual situation. Once you have a clear fantasy in your mind, you will feel your body starting to react. Depending on how you feel about the fantasy, you may experience an increased pulse rate, bodily temperature change and/or emotional responses.

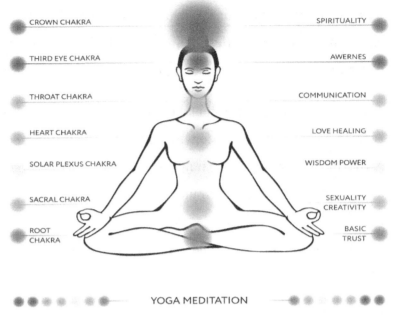

CROWN CHAKRA   SPIRITUALITY

THIRD EYE CHAKRA   AWERNES

THROAT CHAKRA   COMMUNICATION

HEART CHAKRA   LOVE HEALING

SOLAR PLEXUS CHAKRA   WISDOM POWER

SACRAL CHAKRA   SEXUALITY CREATIVITY

ROOT CHAKRA   BASIC TRUST

YOGA MEDITATION

Once you have built up your sexual energy and achieved a state of excitement, begin to move the energy up your body to the higher chakras. Contract your pelvic floor muscles to pump the hormones up into the endocrine system, and make the sound of "Ah" deep from your diaphragm to aid in moving the energy. (The "Ah" sound has been used for centuries as a way to work with the creative energies found in Nature and the Universe to assist in manifesting desires. It is a quantum sound frequency that has been studied and noted to specifically move these energies that are found in the sex center.)

During this process, you will likely experience a tingling sensation in your spine as the energy moves up. Imagine moving the energy from your sacral/creative chakra into your wisdom/solar plexus chakra. While doing this, visualize bright yellow colors and feel your creativity expand. If you have any kind of problem in your life, this is the time to think of creative solutions. However, don't lose your sexual level of responses by focusing too much on the problem. Allow only the solution to drift into your mind and then let it go. Continue with the "Ah" sound to help move the energy.

Step 3

Continue to move this energy upwards and into the heart/love chakra. Begin to perceive the love that you already are. Feel the power of that love and sexual energy combined. Offer loving appreciation for your sexual power and energy. Experience increasing joy and ecstasy as the sexual energy is transmuted into the vibration of love that radiates from you.

Step 4

Continue with the process by moving the sexual energy into the throat/communication chakra. Feel the vibration of the "Ah" sound as it vibrates in your throat – both in the front and the back. This area in the body gives you the power to express your desires. If your sexual energy begins to fade, recall your fantasy as needed to build this energy back up.

Step 5

Bring your sexual energy up to the level of the third eye/awareness chakra. Feel the power of your love and sexual energy in your forehead. Feel it tingle in your back. This is the time to set your intention by visualizing the relationship you desire. Picture it clearly and feel the sensations that correspond. For example: love, intimacy, excitement, adventure, fun. Imagine a loving encounter with your new partner that increases your responses. Direct all of the intense power of this excitement into the visualization within the third eye chakra area. Imagine that your desires are already in place and feel satisfaction in the manifestation.

Step 6

Move this energy once more into your crown/spirituality chakra for the energy of the Universe to connect with it. Clench your pelvic muscles to send bursts of energy up from your sacral chakra to your crown chakra and maintain the state of ecstasy for as long as possible without exhausting yourself. Then gently release this energy from your crown and into the heavens. This "letting go" allows room for your desire to become a physical manifestation.

Sexual energy is near limitless and can be re-directed to turn any person into a manifestation machine. The emotional charge of sexual energy is one of the strongest emotions available to us. When this feeling state is directed into a creative desire, it sends a super-charged vibration into the Universe regarding our intent.

Helpful Hint: This exercise is powerful for any type of creation you'd like to manifest for yourself. Simply reflect on what you'd like to create in your life during step 5 -- work, family, money, good health, intimate relationship, etc. – and create a vivid image of what it looks like.

#40: Exercise – *Acting "As If"*

By pretending to already have the intended desire, it sends a clear message to the Universe that delivery of it is expected. Below are a few ways to act "as if" you're already in the relationship with the partner of your dreams. Through living in this manner as much as possible, there is a deep energetic connection that draws to you that which you already are.

1. Play music that you imagine your partner would enjoy. Dance to the rhythm and/or imagine singing it to your new mate.

2. Dress the part. In other words, what would you wear if this person were on the way to your house? How would you dress to go to sleep next to this person?

3. Wake up every morning imagining your partner next to you. Have an imaginary conversation with them about what the two of you plan to do for the day. Act "as if" you're having a conversation over coffee and bagels.

4. Go to sleep imagining this person next to you every night. How does it feel to be beside them? What types of conversations do you have?

5. Buy greeting cards for your partner's birthday, or to celebrate your anniversary together. Realize that you will be able to use these cards to give to your significant other soon.

6. Fix what you would imagine to be their favorite meal. You can even go as far as lighting some candles and setting the table for two (as long as it doesn't create resistance within you). Or, just imagine what your dinner conversations might be like.

7. Send texts or emails to yourself that might be written by your partner and imagine it coming from them. For example: "I love you. I hope you're having a great day!" Or, "I can't wait to see you later!"

8. When you're out shopping, imagine the things that you might buy for your mate. Pick things up and decide if it would be a good fit for them or not based on their likes and dislikes.

These are just examples. Begin to consider what you could do to generate the feeling that you are already sharing your life with your partner. What are the things that might please them? What are the things they do or say to please you? How would your life together be? What sorts of things would you do? Absorb yourself in the fantasy of living "as if" it's already happening to see the miracle of it being created in your life.

#41: Exercise - *Coloring With Intention*

A mandala is a geometric symbol representing the Universe. It symbolizes unity, harmony and the circle of life. By focusing on a mandala intently, a person is able to connect with enhanced spiritual energy. It stimulates inner peace and healing, as well as creative abilities. This type of exercise is meditative and a superb way to connect with your higher consciousness for manifestation accuracy and solutions to queries. Below this exercise are three mandalas that you can use. Or, there are many of these images available on the internet.

Step 1

Grab multiple colored pencils or markers and choose a mandala that "speaks" to you. Take in all of the beauty of the design and let your mind float away from the race world. This is a time to allow your creative mind to flow through you.

Step 2

You may want to turn on some soothing music, but it is always a good idea to take some deep breaths and relax before you begin. You want to be in state that is free from tension and stress.

Step 3

As you begin coloring the spaces on the mandala, declare your relationship intentions. For example: "I am now finding the perfect spiritual friend and lover to go through life with. My new partner has a great sense of humor and enjoys the same things I do. This person is kind to animals and likes to be out in Nature as much as me. We have so many things in common and always bring out the best in each other. I am so physically attracted to my new partner. This relationship adds tremendous joy to my life and I love every moment of it."

For each intention, use a different color than you did with the previous intention. You may choose to fill in the mandala in one sitting, or come back to it as you create more intentions to add. Once the mandala is complete, you will have a physical testimony of the qualities that you're manifesting regarding your new relationship.

Step 4

Place your mandala somewhere where you might glance at it throughout the day. Your subconscious mind will recall the qualities you've specified by connecting them with the colors you've chosen and endorse the sensations that correspond. This will increase your vibrational level regarding the love you are attracting into your life.

People who spend time concentrating on their intentions while reinforcing them with this action state say that they find clarity and resolution in many other areas as well. This meditative process creates intimacy with feeling states while adding a physical component that strengthens the manifestation, as well as building the neural pathways related to the subject. You may choose to have one mandala solely for the purpose of creating the relationship you desire, or add several of them as you become more and more specific with the details you intend to produce.

Mandala 1

Mandala 2

Mandala 3

7

Neuro-Linguistic Programming

Exercises

Neuro Linguistic Programming incorporates exercises that are based on altering the connection between neurological processes and behavioral patterns. It goes on the premise that behavior is learned through environmental stimulation, and can be unlearned, and re-programmed (if you will), when a person is experiencing less than desirable results in their life.

These processes are highly effective with directly impressing the subconscious mind to eliminate memories of traumatic experiences and phobias that a person may have developed, as well as altering perception and beliefs in order to manifest more desirable outcomes. In other words, if you can identify a belief or impression that is keeping you from creating what you desire, NLP processes are great for effectively eliminating them. The exercises, which center around visualization and sub-modalities (qualities of our thoughts and feelings), are easy to do and usually astonish people with results if dedication is applied towards them.

#42: Exercise - _Changing the Story Your Mind Tells You_

Many people have had a situation where they wanted to do something but the storyteller in their head had different ideas. This storyteller might say, "You're not good enough, "They won't like you," or some other destructive little gem. If you've had this happen to you, this simple and fun exercise will show you how to change your perception of any negative scripts your storyteller is serving you.

Step 1

Think of an occasion where your mind has presented you with a list of reasons that stop you from doing something you really want to do. This list consists of what would be considered insecurities; they are your storyteller's reasons 'why' attempting to do what you really want to do would be futile

Step 2

Notice where this critical storyteller's voice comes from. How does it sound? Is it your voice or is it someone else's? Once you have a clear idea of what the voice sounds like, we're going to change it. Take the time you need to be precise about this.

Step 3

Imagine this same critical voice moving very far into the distance so that you could barely hear it. Now, imagine that it also sounds like

Donald Duck. Add a mouthful of helium to what it's saying for even more fun. Place a musical track from a funny show on top of this voice's criticism. Imagine it coming from a radio station full of static, making it's barely audible. Or, think of any other ways that might distort this script in a fun way.

Step 4

Evaluate how you feel about this voice's disapproval of what you want for yourself. Can you listen to that voice now without laughing? Can you take the voice quite so seriously anymore? Does it have the same impact on you as before?

If this nagging voice still has some influence on you, run it through the process a few more times. Think of funny or unserious ways to alter what it has to say. Make it as ridiculous as possible to alter the meaning of what is being said.

Any time a nagging script is presented to you by your storyteller, you can run it through this process. By doing so, your subconscious mind scratches the record of it in your mind. In other words, it will have a difficult time recalling the seriousness of it in the future, and one by one you will be able to eliminate any negative chatter that stops you from having and doing what you want. Through ceasing this type of story from running in the mind, you create room for new, more positive beliefs that open your life to new, more positive manifestations.

#43: Exercise - _Circle of Confidence_

What could you do with your life if you could access states of confidence, security, certainty, control, or any other positive empowering state you desire literally at will? With these types of states, a person is opened up to new possibilities regarding the freedom they have with people, experiences and personal accomplishments. Think about the areas where your life could be different in wonderfully exciting ways just by possessing supreme confidence.

Many people have places in their life (generally very specific places) where they've felt less than at their very best. Past experiences trigger old wounds that may make a person lack the necessary confidence, certainty, assuredness or other powerful resource states that would make all the difference in the world for them. Imagine what you could accomplish if you had more confidence exactly when you want it.

This exercise will teach you how to literally anchor yourself to your choice of 'state' whenever and wherever you want. It is an amazingly effective process by which it is possible to attach empowering states such as confidence, power, security, control, certainty, or happiness to specific times, places and/or events where you know you'd like to experience them at will. Please allow yourself to be in a quiet, undisturbed space for about 10 minutes to complete this exercise.

142

Step 1

Stand in a relaxed posture, close your eyes and breathe deeply for a few moments. Let your mind go back to a memory of a time when you felt abundantly confident. Step back into that event and experience it fully again. See what you were seeing, hear what you were hearing, recall what you were saying to yourself in that particular situation, and most importantly feel those powerful feelings of confidence moving through your body.

If you find yourself challenged to bring back to your body what you consider to be sufficiently powerful states of confidence, it can sometimes be easier to think about what it's like when you feel totally confident. For example: What are you good at? Where in your life do you feel completely confident? What's it like when you feel confidence? Where in your body do you feel it when you feel that you are ultimately confident? What does it feel like when you feel it? Lastly, how do you know you're feeling confident when you are feeling confident?

If you are still having trouble accessing this feeling state, ask yourself what it must feel like to be the most confident person you know. Choose a person that you believe to have ultimate confidence on every level and step into their shoes for just a few moments. Feel what it feels like to be as self-assured and poised as they are.

Step 2

As you experience the building of confidence inside of you, imagine a colored circle on the floor directly in front of you. What color would you like your circle to be? Would it also have a sound, like a soft hum or a vibration that indicates how powerful it is?

Step 3

When the feeling of confidence is at its peak within you, step forward into your Circle of Confidence and feel the power of this confidence envelope your body. Imagine that it is filling you up, penetrating every cell, pore, tissue, muscle fiber and organ in your body. Breathe deeply and inhale the power and confidence through your nose. Stay in this place until you feel totally at one and completely integrated with your ultimate state of confidence.

Step 4

Once you've accomplished this ultimate state of confidence, step back outside of your Circle and leave those feelings of Confidence remaining inside of the circle. It sounds unusual, but you can do it.

Step 5

Now think of a specific time in your future when you are choosing to experience these same feelings of extreme confidence. See and hear what will be there just before you are choosing to feel these feelings of confidence. The cue could be anything from a business meeting, a job interview, hearing yourself being introduced before a speech, your boss walking into the room, a social gathering or whatever experience you choose.

Step 6

As soon as the visual and auditory cues of this upcoming event are clear in your mind, step back into the circle and feel those grand feelings of confidence well up inside of you once again. Imagine that situation unfolding around you in the future with these confident feelings fully available to you. Take as much time as you need to fully experience the sense of total confidence and control you have over yourself and your environment in the desired situation.

Step 7

Step back out of the circle again, leaving those confident feelings there in the circle. Outside of the circle, take a moment to think again of that upcoming event. Are you able to automatically recall those confident feelings? If so, you've already preprogrammed yourself for tremendous feelings of confidence at that future happening. You're feeling better about it, and it hasn't even happened yet. When it arrives, you'll find yourself responding much more confidently now.

If you're not completely satisfied with the feelings of confidence you now experience, simply repeat the process several more times. After several tries, you should be feeling abundantly confident at the thought of this upcoming event.

The trick to making this exercise work really well depends on the patience you're willing to exercise in discovering how you know when to feel fearful, anxious or uncertain when exposed to the triggers that cause you to do so. Take the time to realize what you're seeing, hearing or feeling that tells you it's time to feel unsure. This is the process of identifying what your specific environmental triggers are.

Questions to keep in mind when finding the triggers you have:

1. Where specifically do you experience a lack of confidence? Are you in your house, the car, a store, around a specific person, at work, a speaking event, etc.?

2. When specifically do you experience this problem? What lets you know that it's time to feel uncertain? Does it happen first thing in the morning? Just before leaving the house? Or, do you experience it at a social gathering?

3. Most importantly, what specifically are you doing right before you get the feelings you don't want? What do you notice in your environment? What might you be looking at, hearing or feeling just before you get the feelings you don't want?

Take time to uncover what has to be there in the "movie" of those times and places wherein you are most likely to create the feelings you don't want. If your anxiety is more of the anticipatory type, you'll begin to notice just what you do inside your head, possibly totally subconsciously, to create the feelings you don't want. Consider the fact that you don't always feel uncertain or unconfident. Somehow, some way, your mind knows when to do it. More than likely, this is due to something you're noticing in your environment, or an external trigger that tells you this is the time to do this uncertainty.

Your job is to identify what it is that you are seeing, hearing or feeling right before you get the feelings you don't want. Use that as your trigger picture for your Circle of Confidence. Once you have your trigger picture, step into your circle to alter the emotional state that is attached.

#44: Exercise - <u>Negative Belief Disintegrator</u>

The purpose of this exercise is to enable you to take a negative belief you hold about yourself, one that you know limits you, and destroy it. By doing so, you add more flexibility and options in your life for creating what you want. It is important to understand the steps so that you can perform this process without any doubt as to what you are doing and why.

A belief change doesn't need any doubt associated with it. Therefore, as well as reading the exercise several times, it is a good idea to try it a few times with a minor belief before attempting it with more significant beliefs that you know are not advantageous to you.

Step 1

Think of something that you do not believe. This does not need to be something important. In fact, something trivial such as the belief that the sky is green or some other minor nonsensical belief is best. Think of this non-belief and notice that when you think of it you visualize something related to it. It might be a picture of a green sky, or something completely different.

Where in your mind or space is that image positioned? Is it to the right? To the left? How far away is it? Do you say anything in your head, or hear any sounds in your mind that tell you that this is not a belief you hold? If so, make a note of them. This is your 'don't believe' position.

Take a moment to think about something completely different like the weather or your last bank statement.

Step 2

Now, think of something that you are not sure whether it's true or not. In fact, pick something that you don't really care about either way. For instance, I don't know if gold is denser than silver, and it certainly doesn't have a particularly major effect on my life either way. Imagine this idea and as before notice that when you think of it you visualize something related to it. Where in your mind or space is that image positioned? Is it to the right? To the left? How far away is it? This is your 'don't care' position.

Step 3

Now that you have two positions, think of a belief you have that you wish to destroy, and notice where that image is in your mind. Take that image and move it into the 'don't care' position. Once you've done that, move it into the 'don't believe' position. If there were any internal sounds connected to the belief you're destroying, repeat them in your head when you position the image into the 'don't believe' position. There are a couple of things that may make this difficult and these are as follows:

1) The image will not move from the left to the right or vice versa. This seems to be a general problem.

The way around this is to move the image into the center, way off in the distance and then pull it forward into the second position from that point. Do this as fast as possible.

2) The image moves back to its original position. There are a number of ways to solve this.

■When you move the image make a sound in your head to swish the image into the new position.

■Imagine an adhesive on the back of the image and stick it in place

■Nail it into place

■Imagine a series of locks that are holding it in place

■Think of any way you could hold the image in place in the real world and imagine it.

Once you have the image in the correct place, make sure that it is the same size as the original.

Test it: Think of something completely different, and then think of the new belief.

How do you feel about it now?

Does it have the correct position and size?

Did you hear the internal dialogue that tells you that you don't believe it?

If not, go back over the steps again.

With this process, which can take practice, the subconscious mind understands the cues given. Think of your computer desktop. If you were to have multiple files on this desktop, they would be designated for different things. Just as your computer has multiple areas to store different types of information, your mind positions items by significance in a similar manner.

For instance, your recycle bin on your desktop might be in the upper left corner, while important financial information might be in the upper right corner. By placing files in the correct position, you are able to access them according to their meaning. In other words, your mind may store beliefs in one position, non-beliefs in another and irrelevant information somewhere completely different. Once you're able to master this process by locating the position, you can remove any beliefs that you feel may be holding you back by placing them in the correct location.

#45: Exercise - *Positive Belief Creator*

The purpose of this exercise is to enable you to create a new belief to give you more options and flexibility in your life. For instance, believing that you experience only good things in your life is a useful belief to create. This process is very similar to the foregoing one with the exception of the fact that you will now be installing a belief of your choice.

Just like the previous exercise, it's important to understand the steps so that you can perform this without any doubt as to what you are doing and why. A new belief doesn't need any doubt associated with it. Therefore, as well as reading the exercise several times, it is a good idea to try the exercise out a few times with a minor belief before attempting it with anything life changing.

Step 1

Think of something that you sincerely believe. This does not need to be something important. In fact, something simple such as the belief that you can breathe, or some other undeniable belief is best. Imagine that belief and notice that when you think of it you visualize something related to it. Where in your mind or space that image is positioned? Is it to the right? To the left? How far away is it? Do you say anything in your head, or hear any sounds that tell you that this is a belief? If so, make a note of them. This is your 'belief' position.

Take a moment to think about something completely different like the weather or your last bank statement. Or, you could just let your mind go blank.

Step 2

Imagine something that you are unsure as to whether it's true or false. In fact, pick something that you don't really care about either way. For instance, I don't know whether big foot really exists or not, but it certainly doesn't have a particularly major effect on my life either way. As before, notice that when you think of this you visualize something related to that idea. Where in your mind or space is that image is positioned? Is it to the right? To the left? How far away is it? This is your 'don't care' position.

Step 3

Now that you have your two image positions, think of the belief you wish to create, and notice where that image is. First, you will need to move the image into the same position as the 'don't care' belief. Secondly, move the new belief image into the 'belief' position. If there were any internal sounds connected to the belief, repeat them in your head when you position the image into the 'belief' position.

As in the previous exercise, if you find it difficult to move the image to the position you wish it to go in, use the following techniques to assist:

1) The image will not move from the left to the right or vice versa.

Move the image into the center way off in the distance so it almost vanishes and then pull it towards you and into the second position. Do this as fast as possible.

2) The image moves back to its original position.

■When you move the image make a sound in your head to swish the image into the new position

■Imagine an adhesive on the back of the image and stick it in place

■Nail it into place

■Imagine a series of locks that are holding it in place

■Think of any way you could hold the image in place in the real world and imagine it

Once you have the image in the correct place, make sure that it is the same size as the original.

Test it: Think of something completely different. Let your mind go blank again, and then think of the new belief.

How do you feel about it now?

Does it have the correct position and size?

Did you hear the internal dialogue that tells you that it's true?

If not, go back and run through the steps again.

#46: Exercise - *How You Create Your Future*

This is a fun exercise that will show you the exact ways you create for yourself. It incorporates visualization with performance to give you an idea of the manner in which your mind has the ability to create what you practice mentally. Through completing this exercise, you reinforce your minds understanding of your ability to create what you desire and imagine for yourself.

Step 1

Stand up, facing straight ahead, with your feet about shoulder-width apart and your knees slightly bent for comfort. Raise your right arm in front of you until it's shoulder height, and point your forefinger straight out in front of you.

Step 2

Keeping your feet planted, rotate your body and your right arm in a clockwise direction and keep turning your body about as far as you comfortably can, noticing how far you can go until you can turn no more. Don't strain yourself, just go as far as you comfortably can and observe where you end up. Take a mental snapshot of whatever it is you're pointing at. When you've done that, come back around again, and return to your original position.

Take a deep breath and close your eyes now.

Step 3

This time, in your imagination only, mentally raise your right arm and forefinger the way you did before. Imagine what it's like to turn your body again in a clockwise direction as far as you can go. But this time, see, hear and feel yourself going even further. In fact, imagine yourself going a full 25% further than you did before!

Notice how in your imagination it feels easy and effortless to turn your body comfortably clockwise a full 25% further than you did previously. Feel as though it were the most natural thing in the world to be able to rotate your body and your hips this easily. When you've done that, take a mental snapshot in your mind's eye of where you end up this time.

Step 4

Now, imagine yourself coming back around again, all the way until your body and your arm are pointing right straight out in front of you once more. Mentally lower your arm until it's back down at your side again.

Take a deep breath. Open your eyes, and then close them again.

Step 5

Once again, in your imagination only, mentally raise your right arm and point your forefinger until it's pointing right straight ahead. In your imagination only, rotate your body in a clockwise direction. See, hear and feel the experience of rotating your body easily, effortlessly and comfortably until you've traveled an additional 25% further than you did just a moment ago! Notice in your imagination that if you wanted to, you could go even further, easily and comfortably!

Step 6

Notice where you end up in your mind's eye; in other words, what you are pointing at? When you've taken a clear mental snapshot of what it feels like to be in this position, go ahead and rotate back around again until your body and your forearm are pointed straight ahead. When you've done that, mentally lower your arm until it's back down at your side once again.

Take a deep breath, open your eyes and them close them again.

Step 7

Just once more, in your imagination only, raise your right arm to shoulder height and point your forefinger right straight ahead. In your imagination only, rotate your right arm and your body in a clockwise direction. Go even further this time than you did before. In fact, imagine turning clockwise a full 360 degrees! Imagine that it feels comfortable, easy and effortless. Notice how good it feels in your hips and your body to be so flexible! Take a mental snapshot of how it feels to be in this position, and when you're sure you've done that, rotate your body back to its original position, with your arm pointing straight ahead again. When you're there, go ahead and lower your arm back down to your side.

Take a deep breath and open your eyes.

Step 8

With your eyes open this time, we'll do the same exercise once more. But this time, perform the gesture physically as in the first steps, rather than mentally. So, again, with your eyes remaining fully open, raise your right arm and point your forefinger right straight ahead. Rotate your right arm and your body in a clockwise direction once again. What happens? If you're like most people, you may realize that you've gone at least a full 25 – 50% further than you did the very first time you tried this!

How did you manage to go so much further this time? The answer to that question is no less than the very secret of creating your future. But, what really happened here?

The most succinct answer is that you ran through the steps of visualization that are required to create desires. You first created a well-defined imagination of a chosen goal state (you decided what you wanted with clarity and specificity), and then stepped into the experience of having that goal state (rehearsed it in your mind) as though it were real for you NOW.

3 Important Steps to Bringing Your Desires into Physical Reality:

1. Decide with clarity and specificity what you want in your life.
2. Create a vivid, sensory-rich visualization of what it would look, sound and feel like if you were living that reality right NOW.
3. Step into (associate with) the experience of the outcome fulfilled, and experience it as though it were really happening.

A person that is able to move into the sensory-rich experience of the goal fulfilled cannot help but set into motion the Universal forces that bring that outcome into fruition. That's what you accomplished in the last exercise; you knew what it was you wanted, and then literally "stepped into" the experience of the outcome fulfilled, feeling just the way it would feel as if you were experiencing that outcome now.

Pay attention to what the results were with this exercise. You spent all of about 5 minutes on the process, and in the matter of those few minutes, chances are you increased your performance by at least 10 – 33%. That's a pretty exciting thing to know when letting your mind wander into the other places in your life where you could use this skill.

During this particular exercise, you didn't increase your inherent abilities; what you really did was install the kinds of resourceful states that would be most likely to lead to the increased performance you experienced. Once you decide with clarity and specificity what you want, you can use your conscious mind to direct your subconscious mind to create the states that correspond in order to manifest it in your life.

#47: Exercise - _Success Conditioning to Manifest Desires_

Behavioral conditioning happens on its own automatically and is just a form of learning. As a human, you are always learning, you can't "not" learn. Every experience, whether monumental or trivial, is a learning experience and generally happens totally subconsciously. Behavioral conditioning is automatic; every time you find yourself automatically stopping at a red light, or running to the phone when it rings, or doing any task that is routine and suddenly realizing you're actually going through the motions of doing it, it is behavioral conditioning.

This also applies to responding with unwanted behavior that keep you from commanding your success. It happens quickly and automatically whenever you see, hear or feel whatever the old triggers use to be; this is a pairing of an emotional or behavioral state (i.e. frustration, distress) with a unique environmental stimulus (a sight, sound, smell, taste or touch of someone or something, or a combination of those). Scientists refer to this kind of pairing between environmental stimuli and behavioral responses as classical conditioning. It happens all of the time for human beings, and is almost always outside of the conscious awareness.

So, how did you learn to pair an environmental stimulus and your response to it? For example, think of how seeing a spinning red light in your rearview mirror gives you a seemingly instantaneous response of moving out of the way. (Most people have an immediate shot of fear that goes through their body when they see this.) We'll answer this by exploring the way behavioral responses are created.

The subconscious mind can associate an array of emotions with sights, sounds or imagination of things happening. Many people will often have no conscious realization of why they're behaving the way they are. This can cause a person to feel as though they are imbalanced; or, they may label themselves as having a mental disorder due only to the fact that they don't know how the human brain works. The truth of the matter is, they are responding this way because their brain works perfectly fine! In fact, it's doing exactly what it was designed to do.

The following exercise is useful in programming your brain to respond in the manner that you want it to the next time you find yourself obstructing what it is you truly desire. You may find some of the steps to be repetitive; however, remember that this is an important part of the process for the mind to establish new behaviors.

Step 1

Take a moment to imagine the type of situation where you've found yourself feeling or behaving negatively in the past that you would like to be responding differently. For example: You may want to be successful and prosperous but can't seem to find the motivation. Or,

161

maybe it's just that you're not sure what direction to take to make this happen for you and you feel frustrated or overwhelmed because of that. More so, you may realize that you're sabotaging your own efforts on a subconscious level and want to change that pattern due to the distress it causes you.

Take your time and notice what it is about the situation that has caused you to feel the way you don't want to feel. What is it that causes you to block yourself? What do you see in this image or setting that isn't present when you're not feeling unmotivated, frustrated or distressed? Run through the experience in your mind as many times as needed in order to help you determine what the subconscious trigger is that causes this behavior. Pay close attention to the point in the scenario in your mind where you really feel your highest level of angst.

Once you've determined what it is that you're seeing when you've been responding in an unwanted way, take a mental snapshot of whatever it is you're looking at. This is called the "negative cue image."

Step 2

Put the "negative cue image" aside temporarily. Clear your mind by saying your telephone number out loud. Next, try saying the alphabet aloud, but in reverse!

Step 3

Now, take a few moments to imagine an image of yourself in the manner you would look if you already had everything you wanted for yourself. Imagine this "you" standing directly in front of you. This is the future you; a you that is just a few steps ahead of you and has already learned how to overcome the challenges that have bothered you in the past.

This you has solved the problem totally with methods that are yet to occur to you, and this you knows that you will succeed because this you already has! This you has already been through everything you've been through, and even a little more. This you thinks of you with love and kindness and knows that you will succeed!

Imagine this "Wonderful You" standing directly in front of you and as a large, bright and colorful image. This you has many resources to handle the behavioral responses that have been a problem for you in the past. This you has many additional choices and a multitude of different ways to get past whatever you previously saw as the "negative cue image." Take a moment to notice how powerfully drawn to this "you" you are, and how just by looking at this other you, you find yourself having the strong feeling of wanting to be just like that person.

Take whatever time you need to make the image as real and believable as possible, making this you a person that you know you want to be. Use the visual qualities of your imagination to enrich this image of you by making the image larger, brighter, more colorful and/or moving. To make your visualization even more compelling, ask yourself, "What if this 'Wonderful You' were powerfully mesmerizing? What would that look like?" This type of "what if" question will immediately allow your brain to create a more intoxicatingly attractive image of the new "Wonderful You."

Step 4

Imagine this new "Wonderful You" shrinking down into a tiny sparkling dot, just as the good witch became in the Wizard of Oz movie. Imagine it as a powerful, concentrated glowing pebble full of all of the wonderful qualities that make a person successful and prosperous in life.

Step 5

Recall once again your "negative cue image," but see it as being a stained glass window in your mind. Have you ever used a slingshot? Think of placing your tiny sparkling dot that contains the new "Wonderful You" into a slingshot. Now, imagine holding the slingshot right out in front of you and pointing directly at you. See yourself pulling it back, away from you, further and further out in front of you until you can feel the tension in the slingshot grow so large that you can't hold it any longer!

Release the slingshot and imagine this tiny sparkling dot, containing the "Wonderful You" coming screaming up at you, growing and expanding, bigger and brighter, until it breaks through the negative cue image and completely destroys it in the process -- just as a pebble would do to a stained glass window. In place of the old image, see the big, bright, colorful, exciting image of the "Wonderful You" and feel the victory as you do so!

Step 6

Open your eyes and close them again to clear the screen.

Step 7

The key to making this exercise a success is speed and repetition. So, we're going to do these steps a bit more quickly now.

Imagine placing the tiny sparkling dot in the slingshot and pulling back the slingshot, away from you...pulling back further and further, until the tension in the slingshot becomes so great, you just have to LET IT GO. The tiny sparkling dot comes screaming up towards you, breaking through the unpleasant image, totally destroying it in the process! In its place is the big, bright, colorful, "Wonderful You!"

Now, take the time to feel this success as you see this amazingly compelling image of the "Wonderful You" fully engage your mental vision!

Open your eyes and close them again to clear the screen.

Step 8

Repeat this step ten more times, being sure to open and then close your eyes again between each time.

Step 9

Now, do the whole process five more times, doing it faster each time, and making sure to see the clear screen in your mind between each time.

Step 10

Ok, I said it would be repetitive. Repeat the process three more times, being sure to see the clear screen between each time.

Step 11

And finally, run the process two more times, as fast you possibly can. Be sure to see the clear screen between each time. When this is completed really fast, you may not consciously be aware of the images as they exchange places.

Step 12

Now that you've run this process LOTS of times, it's important to test the effects of your work. Take a moment to notice what happens when you try to get that original, unpleasant cue image back in mind.

Try really hard to get the old feelings back. You may just find that you cannot.

If by chance you were able to recover any of the old, disempowering feelings, run this exercise 10 to 20 more times, remembering that speed and repetition are the keys to making it work for you.

Behavioral conditioning is a very powerful form of learning. If a person can learn to harness this power and begin to purposefully control and direct it, then the ability for that person to program or condition powerful responses in the manner chosen is an exciting prospect. Anchoring the type of behavioral responses wanted can become a very real response in place of unwanted actions and reactions. The more a person tells their brain what it is that they want, the more likely that person is to experience it automatically. And once this occurs on an internal level, outer circumstances that match will be attracted.

#48: Exercise - *Whiteout Technique*

The purpose of this process is to enable you to stop thinking about a memory that keeps forcing itself into your consciousness, and makes you feel uncomfortable. We all have bad or embarrassing memories that prevent us from performing at our best. This is a simple exercise that is designed to push them out of your awareness for good so that you can remove any blocks that stand in your way of creating what you really want.

Step 1

Think of something that, when you think of it, it makes you feel uncomfortable. This will be something that you know halts you when you attempt to make changes in your life. It will be one of those nagging stories that your mind insists on telling you that causes you to feel insecure about attempting something new.

For instance: Maybe there is something that you can't get out of your mind that produces a negative feeling. Such as, there might be a time when you embarrassed yourself, or a memory that tends to remind you how useless you are at a particular skill, specifically when you are trying to perform at your best.

Get that image clearly in your mind.

Step 2

Place this mental image on a television or movie screen within your mind. Now, imagine that you have the controls for this screen; in particular, your hand is on the "brightness" knob. Turn the brightness to this image up very quickly and all the way to white.

Pause for a moment and think of something completely different like standing on one leg while trying to hula hoop -- to break your state.

Step 3

Think of the memory again. Now, imagine this image again on the screen in your mind. Once again, turn the brightness to this image up VERY quickly and ALL the way to white. Pause for a moment and think of something completely different - - maybe this time, puppies and kittens.

Step 4

Repeat this process, including breaking your state in between, five more times.

Step 5

Think of this unwanted memory again and notice how you feel about it. Hopefully it does one of two things: Either it whites out all by itself (spooky), or you can't visualize the image clearly at all.

By repeating this process over and over you are telling your brain what you want it to do. In finishing each attempt with a completely white image, it makes it very difficult for the brain to reverse the process. The pause between each attempt is important to ensure that you're not creating a loop where your brain just keeps creating the image and brightening it, over and over.

Helpful Hints: If you're still able to feel bad about the image, try repeating the process a few more times. You may want to perform the whiteout quicker, or try adding a sound effect to see and hear your image rush into white for more concrete results.

#49: Exercise – *The Swish Pattern*

This particular process is great to apply to issues of motivation. Similar to the previous process, you will be replacing an unwanted image and related emotional state with a more desirable representation. In this way, you are able to take on the condition of "being" more of what you want to attract to yourself. As mentioned earlier in the book, you don't attract what you want; you attract what you are.

Step 1

Think of an aspect of your life where you are not as resourceful as you would like and notice the representation you make. Perhaps whenever you think about going out for a run you imagine feeling out of breath and not enjoying the experience. Or, you may see yourself as someone that is always "broke," with experiences that directly correspond with that.

Step 2

Now make an image of how you would like to experience that event.

For instance: Form a picture of yourself striding on the treadmill full of energy, with immaculate posture, while all around people are sweating and struggling. Or, imagine yourself going on a shopping spree and freely spending money while you travel from store to store in your brand new car. Remember, this is your representation, so

170

make it as motivating as possible. Take your time to associate the feelings that match this new image of you.

Step 3

When you are happy with this representation, take a break for a moment and think about the original, un-resourceful image and place a small dot in either the center or one of its corners. This small dot is a very small copy of the second (resourceful) image.

Step 4

Now, very quickly, and with a nice whooshing noise, expand the dot until it fills the whole original image -- replacing the old image with the new resourceful one. The positive image should now be the only image you can see. Pause for a moment and think of something different to break your state. For instance: Imagine cats chasing dogs.

Step 5

Return to the first image again. Keep performing this shift until you can complete it effortlessly. Take special care to first imagine the dot and then expand it quickly. Repeat this process 5 more times, remembering to take a mental break between each attempt.

Step 6

Think of the performing task that you had difficulty being resourceful with. What image pops into your mind? Are you able to see the new resourceful image? If not, repeat the process several more times; try to increase the speed in which you transition the images and make your sound effect louder to cause a permanent switch of the images.

The swish pattern can be used to replace any negative thought with a more positive one. As with many NLP techniques, the key is in the speed that you make the change. In addition, by repeating these processes over and over you are consciously telling your subjective mind what you want it to do in a language that it can understand. Once it takes the cue, it will automatically remember the desired result when recalling the image or scenario attached. In this way, you are able to clothe yourself in the state of being required to bring more of those desires into your life.

8

Manifestation Formula

#50: *<u>The Trick to Manifestation</u>*

When it comes to creating what you want in life, the basic steps remain true for all categories. This seven step process is comprised of the practical details that will manifest everything you desire in life. You've undoubtedly used this process, quite possibly unconsciously, to create your current conditions, circumstances and physical objects. However, as earlier stated, on a conscious level it's often easier said than done. Acknowledge this process whenever possible and combine it with the practice of the chosen exercises provided in this book to reinforce your accuracy. With consistency and dedication, you may find yourself attracting everything you've ever wanted from life.

Step 1

Imagine something that you want; something you truly desire to have. The desire to have it accomplished is a very important detail. Remember: The larger the goal, the bigger the desire should be in order to match its significance in your mind and vibration.

Step 2

Travel forward into the future with your mind and experience that this manifestation has happened already. Recall how you feel about this creation. See how happy you are with it and attempt to experience it in a very real and sensory-rich way so that the mind believes in it being factually sound. It's imperative to reach a point, through regular visualization and feeling states, where your belief in this role is absolute; you must inhabit it completely.

Imagine how you feel about this creation. Feel how grateful you are that you have it NOW and how grateful you are that you demonstrated to yourself that you could change your world by mastering your mind. Gratitude is of utmost importance as it is an emotional signature of something that has ALREADY happened. The Universe understands this and corresponds.

Feel how this creation just fell into place and how it's just part of your life experience now. Feel how relaxed you feel knowing that time is no longer important because you already have your desire. Remind yourself of the feeling associated with the day you received this magnificent gift that you created. Feel how right it feels that you designed having it and how it's just part of your life experience now. Fill your mind with details about the feeling of having it and the sense of accomplishment it gives you. Feel how you were able to use your success to inspire you to greater success. Stay here and think about it until you feel how absolute it is. This step is essential to your success.

Step 3

Ask yourself if you really need this to happen in your reality? Your desire has just become real to you, so it's actually real. You've, in fact, already created it. Do you still need it now that it's real? Can you feel why you don't still need it? The feeling you should be experiencing is one of, "Well, this is clearly going to happen in the right time and in the right way. It will occur when it's best for it to occur." This is the feeling you're looking to have in your mind; a very relaxed, calm position regarding your desire, and faith that it has already been created.

This is the miraculous formula: Attachment and detachment of your desire at exactly the same time. It shows your subconscious mind what you want, without pressure -- in a very cool and relaxed way. Anything that you've attained in life, you've achieved with this feeling and mindset before it became yours.

Step 4

Take appropriate action toward your goal. With each thing you want to achieve, seek to become an authority on the subject. Fill your mind with exploration regarding your desire. Take the time to randomly pull up the feeling states related to having this desire, without making it a chore to do so. Make it your goal to put some action into this manifestation daily; even small action will draw this creation closer to you.

For example: If you wanted to make more money, review all of your options for doing so. What would be the best path for you as an individual to take to create more money in your life? What other possibilities have you never considered before? How many different ways could this become a reality for you? If you're seeking a new relationship, begin noticing all of the people you pass by every day. What features are you looking for in a partner? How would they treat you? What type of lifestyle would they live? This prompts your mind seek out the qualities you desire most regarding your goals.

Gather information needed to make your manifestation as precise as possible. Use the exercises given in the prior chapters to prompt your mind and reinforce your abilities. When the brain begins to search for these details, it won't stop until it finds them. Imagine that your job is to come up with all of the ingredients to a recipe; everything that you specifically like. And it's the Universe's job to cook it up for you.

Step 5

Make the conscious goal to be determined and strong willed until this manifestation shows up. Realize that it's going to happen in the best way and in the best time for you. It's already real in your mind and feelings, so it's already yours. Like a child, anticipate how exciting this gift is! Consider what you still may need to learn for all of this to happen. This opens the mind to search further for the answers and in turn draw those answers to you.

The goal is to add less effort and more reflection to the subject. Think of it as a research project that you're gathering information on. Take breaks from it when it feels like a job or duty to diminish resistance; return to it when you're feeling your full potential. Observe how you feel and notice any doubts that show up. Use the NLP exercises given to shut those nagging uncertainties down.

Step 6

Stack the odds in your favor to go from possibility to probability. Remember that you can't give up on something that's already happened to you in your mind and in your feeling states. Once it's real to you, it's already yours. If you can think it up, it's already created as a possibility.

Start with small things that help convince you of your power to manifest. The confidence this builds helps you dare to dream bigger, which convinces your mind further in your ability to create what you desire. Once again, go back to the previous exercises and work on lesser creations that you don't have as much of an attachment to in order to prove to yourself and your mind that your abilities are powerful.

Tell yourself that the entire Universe supports you and wants to please you. Consistently remind yourself that you are a Powerful Creator. Use what works best for you, and try one manifestation at a time. Have fun and make it playful. Time doesn't matter. Success is something you will attain.

Step 7

Strive to serve and help others with your creations. Notice how your manifestations bring good to the world. See how everyone around you is able to benefit from your creations. Through doing this, you give those creations more power. See how others' lives are made easier from your specific gifts. Observe the benefit in your service to others. Fill your mind with the good you bring to people's lives.

By serving others, you will receive any rewards you seek. You are adding to the world with your specific talents. Look to give more as often as possible. Begin to notice how you always receive more than you can give out. Always be open to greater manifestations. This is living in an abundance state, which will create abundance in all areas of your life.

For more law of attraction information, subscribe to our youtube channel at https://www.youtube.com/c/youryouniversechannel

Happy Manifesting!

Made in the USA
Middletown, DE
10 November 2021